Transcending Gender
The Male/Female Double
in Women's Fiction

Challenging the Literary Canon

Other Titles in This Series

The Witch and the Goddess in the
Stories of Isak Dinesen:
A Feminist Reading
Sara Stambaugh

Transcending Gender
The Male/Female Double
in Women's Fiction

by
Joanne Blum

U·M·I Research Press

Ann Arbor / London

Produced and distributed by
UMI Research Press
an imprint of
University Microfilms Inc.
Ann Arbor, Michigan 48106

Library of Congress Cataloging in Publication Data

Blum, Joanne, 1954-
 Transcending gender : the male/female double in women's fiction /
by Joanne Blum.
  p. cm.—(Challenging the literary canon)
  Bibliography: p.
  Includes index.
  ISBN 0-8357-1886-7 (alk. paper)
  1. Fiction—Women authors—History and criticism. 2. Androgyny
(Psychology) in literature. 3. Doubles in literature. 4. Women in
literature. 5. Men in literature. I. Title. II. Series.
PN3426.W65B58   1988
823'.009'353—dc19   88-15592
                                                              CIP

British Library CIP data is available.

34.95

58/54

To Betty Dascomb Blum,
whose model of independence, vitality, and faith
has made all the difference

Contents

Preface

Once upon a time, so the Hans Christian Andersen story goes, an evil demon created a magic mirror which distorted the image of everything it reflected. What was beautiful appeared grotesque; what was ugly looked very large and important. One day this mirror shattered into a million pieces, and wherever the pieces fell, human misery was the result. "The Snow Queen" tells the story of what happened when two of these evil shards of glass fell into the eye and heart of a boy named Kay.

Kay's best friend is a girl named Gerda who lives next door. Their houses are so close together that in the summer they seem to be joined at the top by the branches of the rose trees. Though Kay and Gerda are not really brother and sister, they feel as if they are so; and they look it as well, both having long golden hair and sparkling eyes. They relish each other's company, playing games together, listening to their grand-mothers' stories, enjoying the bloom of the roses, sharing what is in their hearts.

Then Kay is stricken by the demon's magic glass. The piece that falls into his eye makes everything seem ugly: in the roses now he sees only worms. The piece that falls into his heart has the effect of ice, making his heart grow gradually colder and colder. Now his grand-mother's stories strike him as silly and childish, and time spent with Gerda seems an uninteresting distraction from playing with the older boys. Gerda does not understand and grieves at the loss of his spirit.

One day, while out playing with the village boys, Kay hitches his sled to the back of a carriage driven by a beautiful woman dressed all in white. Before even thinking to protest, he discovers his sled is stuck fast, and he is being taken out through the village gates, far into the north. Because of the icy shard lodged in Kay's breast, the Snow Queen has him in her power.

Gerda searches far and wide for Kay, telling her story to every living thing in hopes that one among them can direct her path. She shares her story with the flowers, the river, the prince and princess, a friendly crow and his crow fiancee. In exchange, they tell Gerda their stories, which are—from the princess to the lily-of-the-valley—about connections, and the tragedy of broken connections. Everywhere she goes, other beings empathize with Gerda's story and try to help, even those who themselves live in isolation. Even the lonely robber-girl identifies with Gerda's quest, loaning her a pet reindeer for the cold journey north. From Kay and Gerda's green village to the wild north of Lapland, it is female beings who are most aware of the importance of her quest for reunion.

Barefoot, alone, and without apparent defenses, Gerda nevertheless carries great power with her, power to enlist the service of nature through her storytelling. All hear her words and respond to the tragedy of separation they perceive by directing her course. Guided by the story of the robber-girl's reindeer, Gerda makes her way to the far north where Kay is imprisoned in the Snow Queen's icy palace. Upon meeting the Queen's ice guard, Gerda speaks a prayer for protection, and her warm breath melts them into helplessness.

Kay, alone in the palace, is trying to win his freedom by piecing together the geometric shapes of ice crystals into the word "eternity." The Snow Queen has promised his release if he can form this word, but he cannot in isolation. Kay has given the Snow Queen power over him because of the ice lodged in his heart and his therefore distorted vision of the world. When Gerda at last finds him within the vast rooms of the palace, she melts the piece of ice in Kay's heart with her hot tears; and then Kay's own tears dislodge the other shard from his eyes. They are united, and the ice crystals, after dancing in joy at their reunion, settle down into the shape of eternity which Kay had so long struggled to find with his reason.

Their bond restored, Kay and Gerda are free to leave the Snow Queen's palace and return home. Everywhere they go, people rejoice and the land flourishes. The robber-girl, on her own solitary trek to the north, is happy to see her friend's journey successful, but she questions whether Kay deserved such trouble. Gerda merely pats her head and asks after the welfare of the prince and princess and the crow and his crow-betrothed, implying the deserving is not the point. The point is the necessity of reunion, whatever it takes to sustain it, and whoever must make the effort.

The story of Kay and Gerda in Andersen's "The Snow Queen" provides an image of male/female relationship, and a sense of purpose, which I see expressed in a number of women's fictions. Many female fiction writers seem to be aware of the necessity of connection, as they repeatedly present images—albeit fleetingly at times—of male and female connections which defy the divisions imposed by culture.

This image goes beyond androgyny, as it does in Kay and Gerda's story. The male and female selves are more than opposite, but complementary, gender identities which must be combined for true selfhood to be possible for each. They are intimately connected selves, sharing the same human consciousness, but tragically separated by the gender-distorted roles of culture. Kay and Gerda seem to reflect the stereotypical characteristics traditionally assigned to each sex—masculine logic and reason, feminine intuition and emotion—yet they are also complete, independent selves. And their relationship is characterized more by similarities than differences. Their emergence from a shared space, the boundaries between their self-houses blurred by the lush growth of nature, their similarity in appearance: all suggest that connection is more important for selfhood than separation, and finally that selfhood and relationship are virtually indistinguishable.

So it is in the world, these writers seem to be saying. Gender roles are real constraints imposed by culture, but they are also a distorted mask covering a more basic connection, like the evil magic mirror which the demon of "The Snow Queen" took all over the world to make everyone miserable by its perverted reflections of human life. As culture has been constructed for us, the importance of human connections has been made to seem very trivial indeed. All the ugly forces which divide us, and particularly that central division between men and women, have been made to seem enormous and irreconcilable. And perhaps they are within the ordinary social world (or so at least some writers seem to have concluded). Repeatedly, though, women writers of fiction have tried to construct a space and a model of relationship in which it is possible to get beyond such divisions and to re-establish that possibly mythic, but still perceptibly real, consciousness of connection. As for Gerda in "The Snow Queen," the power of storytelling is the vehicle for this pursuit of connection.

These fictions represent an impulse to transcend the divisions of gender and the distorted images of self and relationship which accompany them. They suggest an awareness of the need for a context—and the works examined here imply various and imaginative methods of supplying one—in which those fragments of the demon's magic mirror can be gotten out of our eyes and an image of wholeness and connection brought into view.

Introduction

Sandra M. Gilbert and Susan Gubar, in *The Madwoman in the Attic*, discuss the imaginative techniques nineteenth-century women authors developed to overcome confinement by gender and to cope with what these critics call "anxiety of authorship" (part 1, chapter 2). The "madwoman" double motif which Gilbert and Gubar examine is the female writer's attempt to unify the fragmented images of female selfhood (the "angel in the house" described by Woolf, the Eve-like seductress, and so on) which are always, to some extent, internalized by women, and to exorcise them so that she may tell her own story. The function of this female double is to act out the anxiety and rage against gender confinement which are repressed in the central female character. These critics have demonstrated that this female double is a significant image in the female literary tradition. I believe there is another double represented in women's fiction, however, which is a response to the same kind of cultural confinement by gender, but which reflects a very different type of effort.

The double motif with which I am concerned is a male/female one, an image of male/female relation which reflects an effort to transcend traditional gender roles.[1] This double is, I believe, another significant method by which female authors have sought to overcome the gender confinement imposed by patriarchal culture. This image of male/female relation can be described as a productive interaction in which the male and female selves overreach their culturally prescribed gender identities to relate to one another in such a way that the boundary between self and other becomes blurred. Male and female become less separate identities (though they remain this as well), more extensions of one another's selfhood, in defiance of the divisions of gender.

This model of male/female interaction cannot be defined as "androgynous," though it partakes of some of the characteristics of androgyny. A number of feminist critics have examined the problems and limitations of the concept of androgyny, primarily based on its subtle reinforcement of gender polarity.[2] While proponents of androgyny posit a transcendence of overly masculine or feminine behavior through a blend, or a combination, of gender-related characteristics, the bipolar construct on which this androgynous blend is based remains firmly intact. Some psychologists have begun to reassess the value of androgyny and to propose a less dichotomous and more "multidimensional" model for human behavior, but this research is only beginning.[3] The model of selfhood and relationship which some women writers are representing in their fictions, either consciously or unconsciously, reflects what psychologists are just beginning to explore: an awareness of human personality and behavior as too complex for definition by gender. The type of female/male double apparent in fictions by the Brontës, Woolf, Laurence and others is a dynamic interaction between male and female which, rather than effecting an androgynous blend of masculine and feminine, defies and transcends these gender constructs.

This male/female double also differs significantly from the way in which the double has traditionally been represented and examined in literary theory. The first and perhaps most easily defined difference concerns the traditional sexual identification of the double. It is, of course, important to note that the tradition of the double has been largely a male one: authors noted for their use of the doppelgänger include Dostoevsky, Poe, Stevenson, and Conrad; and the type of double reflected in their texts is, almost without exception, a single-sexed one. Although there are numerous examples of intimate relationships between men and women in men's fiction, there are few representations of a true male/female double. Several male writers (perhaps most notably Hawthorne and James) appear to approach this image, but, more often than not, the male/female interaction presented in these works does not involve authentic intersubjectivity.

Beyond this difference in sexual identification, however, there is also a significant difference in the nature of the double which recurs in women's fiction, a distinction which is best defined in relation to what I have called intersubjectivity. While critics' definitions of the double have varied considerably throughout its long tradition, they do not in general imply the type of psychological reciprocity, or intersubjectivity, which I see as a definitive characteristic of the male/female double of women's fiction. Usually the term "double," or "doppelgänger," is used to denote a kind of ego-division or fragmentation of self into dual, and sometimes multiple, personalities. In general, one self is the more "realistic" character, the self with whom the reader identifies, and the other remains, to some extent, a "shadow self" which may exert either positive or negative influences on the first self. This second self, or shadow self, most often represents a repressed aspect of the first self, a physical acting-out of buried asocial behaviors, or simply of feelings, beliefs, or actions which the first self cannot express as his/her own. The double need not be physically embodied; it may be only a hallucinatory projection of some aspect of the self (as, for example, in Oscar Wilde's *The Picture of Dorian Gray*). Or it may appear to have both physical existence and independent motives (as in Conrad's "The Secret Sharer"). Often the physical reality of the double is left intentionally ambiguous, as in Dostoevsky's "The Double." In any case, whether it be hallucinatory or realistic, the traditional double implies some kind of psychic fragmentation which is projected from the troubled mind outward into the world.[4]

While, as I have noted, there are many examples of single-sex doubles in women's fiction which can be characterized in ways similar to the above, the male/female double with which I am concerned functions quite differently. In the male/female double bond, one self does not necessarily take precedence over the other, nor can one self be usefully considered as a representation of some aspect of the other. Both are complete selves which, through their interaction with one another, transcend gender identity to attain a deeper awareness both of selfhood and of relationship.

Before examining various representations of the male/female double in women's fiction, it is necessary to look briefly at some of the reasons why female writers seem to demonstrate this capacity for self-projection beyond the boundaries of gender more so than male writers. I believe this ability is firmly rooted in the distinctive qualities of female psychological development as well as in the effects of women's historically oppressed social situation.

To take the latter of these first, it has long been recognized by sociologists that members of oppressed groups exhibit common behavioral and psychological characteristics as a response to oppression. Frequently these characteristics are described as defense strategies or as ways of protecting and sustaining self in an insecure and threatening social environment. Albert Memmi's research in the late Sixties on minority behavior contributed importantly to our understanding of the politics of oppression. One of the central points made by Memmi is that the oppressed group tends to identify with and, to some extent, internalize the attitudes of the dominant group. While a detailed discussion of the validity of comparisons between the social situation of minority groups and of women is beyond my present purpose, certain connections are obvious; certainly the linked history of the early feminist and abolitionist movements in the United States makes this evident. In a now dated but still significant contribution to feminist theory, Helen Hacker first made the important connection between women and other oppressed groups, emphasizing what can be learned about women by studying them in this context. She notes that "women often manifest many of the psychological characteristics which have been imputed to self-conscious minority groups" (61). She discusses, for instance, the tendency of women, as well as of minorities, toward "group self-hatred," or toward identifying with the dominant group and against both other members of the oppressed group and themselves. Thus women often accept the dominant group's stereotyped conceptions of them and denigrate, or mistrust, other women.[5] Essentially a system of scapegoating, of blaming the victim, and of misperceiving the locus of power is at work in this aspect of the politics of oppression. Hacker's comparisons between minorities and women in relation to the types of "accommodation attitudes" they develop as a response to oppression are also particularly relevant. In effect, as a means of survival, oppressed groups invest a good deal of time in studying the dominant group so as to learn how best to influence it or to attain/sustain its good favor.

It is not difficult to see how the development of such accommodation attitudes and habits of identifying with the dominant group, which Hacker and Memmi discuss, could foster in women a capacity for perceiving the thoughts, needs, and expectations of others beyond what is usual for men, because less important for them. If one's comfort, security, even survival, are dependent on the moods of others, it is undoubtedly an important skill to be able to anticipate those moods. Women have traditionally put a good deal more effort into understanding men than men have of women, and the fact that women's survival has frequently depended on this skill is no small part of the reason for its development.

Recent work on female psychological development—and how it has been both misrepresented and ignored by male theorists—also helps to explain women writers' apparently greater capacity for transcending gender in their fictions. Nancy Chodorow, Jean Baker Miller, and, most recently, Carol Gilligan have all examined the ways in which female psychological development differs from male development and, thus, from the male-dominated theory which describes it. Miller, for instance, describes as a "fundamental organizing principle" in women's lives their urge to "stay with, build on, and develop in a context of attachment and affiliation with others" (82–83). Women's sense of self resides in a network of affiliation, frequently to the point, Miller claims, where loss of affiliation may threaten loss of self.

Seeking to discover the psychological effects on men and women of the fact that "women mother," and to see how these effects reproduce themselves generation to generation, Chodorow uncovered findings related to female connectedness and affiliation. Basing her research to some extent on that of the object-relations theorists, who posit that a primary sense of self is established before the age of three, she offers a reinterpretation of male-biased psychoanalytic research, specifically the Freudian oedipal theory, and its differentiated effects on masculine/ feminine development. Women's mothering, she asserts, "produces asymmetries in the relational experiences of girls and boys as they grow up, which account for crucial differences in feminine and masculine personality, and the relational capacities and modes which these entail" (169).

According to her reinterpretation of Freudian oedipal theory, Chodorow explains that the girl's long preoedipal attachment to her mother (the length of which concerned Freud because he saw this as causing a delay in feminine maturation) sets the stage for a different inner and relational sense of self from that of boys. "Mothers tend to experience their daughters as more like, and continuous with, themselves" and correspondingly, girls "tend to remain part of the dyadic primary mother-child relationship itself." By contrast, boys are experienced by their mothers as separate and different from themselves and thus are engaged in a more decisive process of individuation and curtailment of primary bonds. As a result, Chodorow claims, girls emerge from the oedipal situation "with a basis for 'empathy' built into their primary definition of self in a way that boys do not" (166–67). Girls come to perceive themselves as less differentiated than boys and as more continuous with others.

Building on the work of Chodorow and Miller, but focusing specifically on the area of morality and value formation, Carol Gilligan has also examined women's sense of connectedness and empathy. It is Gilligan's work which is most helpful in providing a theoretical context for the male/female double which recurs in women's fiction. Gilligan's research includes: interviews with male and female children, utilizing Kohlberg's moral dilemmas; a rights-responsibility study focusing on women's abortion decisions; and comparison and analysis of the violence content of stories male and female college students ascribed to pictures.

Based on her comparisons of male/female responses in these studies, and building on traditional developmental theory, Gilligan found that men's and women's conceptions of themselves and of morality differ in fairly consistent and significant ways. Men see themselves as more separate and autonomous than women see themselves, and their conception of morality is based on a concern with individual rights and protection from infringement by others. Moral decisions are most often arrived at through logic, by comparison of conflicting individual rights, and by reference to rules designed to monitor such conflicts. By contrast, women perceive themselves more in relation to others and thus perceive of morality more from a basis of connection. Morality, for women, emerges less from a focus on rights than from a concern for responsibilities to self and others. Decisions are influenced by the desire not to hurt, to facilitate and sustain relationships, and to foster communication. Women's much-touted anxiety over competition (as, for instance, in the "Cinderella complex") is, in fact, a reflection of this greater concern with relationships and responsibility to others, misunderstood because it is out of place within a male-biased social environment (a masculine bias which traditional developmental theorists support). Gilligan's violence study revealed that men perceive more danger in connection than in separation, whereas women perceive situations of isolation as most dangerous.

Because of the different dynamics of attachment and separation which males and females experience in the development of gender identity, and their different perceptions of identity and intimacy, Gilligan finds that "male and female voices typically speak of the importance of different truths, the former of the role of separation as it defines and empowers the self, the latter of the ongoing process of attachment that creates and sustains the human community" (156). Since it is women's voices which have most often not been heard, Gilligan suggests that clearly much can be gained from learning to hear them—by the theoreticians as well as by society at large. Consistent with her view that women perceive moral and social realities within a web, or a network, of relationships and responsibilities, Gilligan is not saying that women's sense of self and the world is superior to that of men. Rather, she is suggesting that men and women see and speak differently, and that much can be gained from recognizing and appreciating this difference: women about the necessity of avoiding the trap of self-sacrifice and including self in that network of responsibilities, men about the importance of sustained connection in human life.

This emphasis on affiliation as it has been fostered in female development is a significant reason behind women writers' apparent capacity for transcending gender in their fictions to perceive and identify with the other as a separate, yet very much related, self. In the male/female double figures they create, we can see this process of self-projection and cross-gender connection at work, and frequently the basis of interaction seems directly in line with the model of mutual recognition and gain

Gilligan proposes. Most often these fictions represent men learning from women, striving to define themselves, and to relate to others, in expanded ways made possible by hearing women's different voices— voices which speak of artificial divisions and of sustained connections with others. Like Gilligan, these women fiction writers suggest that the female voice is more often unheard, and is thus the voice from which more can be learned. Some fictions, though, make clear also what women may learn from men which may assist them in self-definition and in self-determination. As the Andersen fairy tale suggests, the crucial matter is not who effects the reunion, but that reunion is achieved.

Although the fictions I will discuss are primarily by twentieth-century female authors, I begin with Emily Brontë's *Wuthering Heights* and Charlotte Brontë's *Jane Eyre*. These two novels effectively describe both the ideal image of cross-sexual bonding (i.e., the male/female double) being pursued in women's fiction and the fundamental obstacles to this bond which emerge when it is socially placed. The different contexts in which the male/female relationships of these novels are situated—Catherine and Heathcliff's bond being situated more within a mythic realm, Jane and Rochester's occupying a very clearly delineated social place— define, in effect, the central conflict modern women writers still face: that transcendence of gender is most feasible in mythic or apatriarchal space and is only partially feasible within the social milieu. The male/ female double, and the transcendence of gender it requires, seems to necessitate extra-social placement, because it challenges the very foundation of social structure.

In the mythic context of *Wuthering Heights*, the boundaries of identity—for Catherine and for Heathcliff—overlap and interfuse, their interconnection so intense that one self has the sense of being, at times, also the other self. That the spiritual bond is broken on the social level, each character reverting to traditional gender roles, reflects Brontë's awareness of the impracticability of this type of male/female communion in the "real" world.

Charlotte Brontë, in *Jane Eyre,* attempts to place this image of male/ female bonding within a social context, to posit an egalitarian marriage which defies gender roles and which allows full humanness to both female and male. Those moments of almost telepathic communication between Jane and Rochester, particularly in the concluding chapters of the novel, suggest the same kind of shared consciousness epitomized in Catherine and Heathcliff. Yet an exacting price is paid for the ideal union described at the conclusion of the novel, and the way toward it involves tremendous difficulties. Jane and Rochester must deal with the obstacles posed by sexual politics, by the inequitable social roles of men and women, and the ways in which those roles have been psychologically internalized to their detriment. In effect, though Jane and Rochester glimpse, from the start, the kind of egalitarian bond they desire, they must struggle to transcend both the external and the internal divisions fostered by gender. This struggle to cross the gender barrier best defines the general development of this narrative; it defines as well the central conflict with which modern writers pursuing this image of bonding must still contend.

Twentieth-century female authors attempting to situate this image of heterosexual connection within some kind of social place have dealt even more consciously (given the modern awareness of gender) with the conflicts social placement entails. Though often their expressions of the male/female double appear to be compromises, or dilutions, of the ideal bond as represented by Emily Brontë, such writers have invariably found unique and creative ways of approaching this transcendent connection.

Virginia Woolf's *Mrs. Dalloway*, for example, pursues this image of interconnectedness on the psychological plane, Woolf using her "stream of consciousness" technique to link the psyches of central male and female characters. That Woolf, in her original conception of the novel, intended only one central character, Clarissa Dalloway, and then developed this character into two selves, Clarissa and Septimus Warren Smith, reflects the magnitude of her interest in an image of consciousness-sharing, or psychological reciprocity, between male and female. On the conscious level, and the social level, Woolf very clearly sees male and female as separate, even, to an extent, antithetical selves. Though interested in finding a space where male and female may merge and connect, she represents (like Emily Brontë) no possibility for this on the level of social interaction. The difficulties of sexual politics defined by Charlotte Brontë are, to the twentieth-century consciousness, even more profound. If gender is to be transcended and male and female to meet as one, it must be on the level of the unconscious, of the psyche, a place below and beyond the daily social sphere.

The contemporary English author, Margaret Drabble, pursues a similar image of female-male connection, but very much within conventional social space. In *The Needle's Eye*, Drabble, like Woolf, represents romantic interaction as destructive of bonding, but she also describes a uniquely dynamic male-female friendship. Although Rose and Simon's relationship is constructive and nurturing for both, Simon is much more in a position of learning about, even redefining, himself and his relationships with others in relation to Rose's example than she from his. Very much in line with Gilligan's theory, Simon profits from Rose's example of intimacy and of sustained connections with others. In a sense, what Simon learns from Rose is what Septimus might have learned from Clarissa had they ever had the opportunity to interact.

Canadian writer Margaret Laurence seems, in *The Diviners*, to approach Gilligan's hypothesis from the other side, in relation to what women may learn from men. Jules Tonnerre's role in the narrative as "male muse" for Morag Gunn, assisting in the process of self-definition and expression for the female artist, suggests that bonding with the male can be self-enabling. Though their bond is a tenuous one, acted upon only infrequently, it plays a pivotal role in the development of the central female artist's sense of self. The implication of this narrative—very much in keeping with Woolf's aesthetic image of the "androgynous mind"—is that creative expression requires transcendence of gender, for female as well as male. Unlike the double relationships explored by most of the other women writers mentioned, the male/female bond portrayed in Laurence's novel includes sexual/romantic interaction. This is something of a rarity in modern literature since, more often than not, sexual involvement appears to complicate human interaction rather than to enhance it, and usually to reinforce gender confinement. As Annis Pratt has pointed out, much more often than not, successfully reciprocal and egalitarian relationships between men and women in fiction occur in "apatriarchal space," that is, outside the social environment.[6] The difficulty of making this image of male/female bonding a social reality has prompted numerous women writers to abandon the social sphere altogether.

Some recent women's science fiction and fantasy has, in many ways, provided a context for this pursuit of a social space in which men and women can interact fully without gender restrictions. The issue of gender has, in fact, been a central concern of many of these writers, perhaps most notable of whom is Ursula Le Guin. She described her novel, *The Left Hand of Darkness*, on one level at least, as an experiment she conducted to find out what would happen to our conception of humanness if gender were completely eliminated. Thus, she constructs an imaginary culture which is totally free of gender roles because there is absolutely no physiological sex distinction. Le Guin is trying to define, in other words, "the area that is shared by men and women alike" (153). The friendship between the Earth ambassador, Genly Ai, and the Gethenian, Estraven, can be characterized, like the doubles of more "realistic" fiction, as an intimate and reciprocal interaction between two selves which, almost literally here, transcends gender constructs.

The utopian community Dorothy Bryant depicts in *The Kin of Ata Are Waiting for You* reflects a similar interest in providing a social space where gender—as well as numerous other cultural divisions—may be transcended. Like Genly Ai's experience with the Gethenian Estraven, the central male character's transformative growth, primarily through his interaction with the female protagonist, Augustine, best defines the central action of the narrative. By means of the challenge to assumptions posed by the Atans and his "double" bond with Augustine, the male character emerges into a deeper and more compassionate attitude toward the human community than had ever been possible within conventional social space.

James Tiptree Jr.'s novel, *Up the Walls of the World*, extends the effort to transcend divisions to its fullest extent, representing not only transcended gender, but also time, distance, species, even galaxies. The image of unified, space-borne consciousness (composed of Earth, Tyree, and computer essence) which concludes the novel is perhaps the purest and most elaborate example of the healing of divisions possible in the realm of science fiction.

Such efforts on the part of recent women writers of fantasy and science fiction to envision a mode of human interaction which is not characterized by gender division (or by other cultural divisions) can be interpreted, in a sense, as a movement back into the mythic world of Emily Brontë, yet with an important distinction: these writers take with them a modern consciousness of gender and of the tremendous degree to which society channels, categorizes, and restricts human behavior based on sexual identification. They carry with them also a clear sense of the necessity that we expand our understanding of what it means to be human.

Within a cultural environment which persists in defining human identity and behavior according to gender norms, this recurrent image of male/female bonding in the fiction of women writers strikes me as both significant and encouraging. It suggests that female fiction writers, despite whatever species of cultural oppression, continue to envision a mode of human interaction which transcends social barriers. It represents a recurrent image of human behavior and interaction which renders "gender schema" theory irrelevant and invalid, and it suggests an ongoing effort toward integration and transcendence of the dichotomous categories according to which we have traditionally defined ourselves. What is perhaps most significant, and even more surprising, about this model of heterosexual interaction is that it should persist despite overwhelming evidence in women's—and men's—literature of the failure of male/female relationships.

The Myth and the Reality in
Wuthering Heights and *Jane Eyre*

It is as if I had a string somewhere under my left ribs, tightly and
inextricably knotted to a similar string situated in the correspond-
ing quarter of your little frame . . . . I am afraid that cord of
communion will be snapped; and then I've a nervous notion I
should take to bleeding inwardly.

Jane Eyre

Emily Brontë and Charlotte Brontë provide alternative but correlative
views of the male/female double, which define both the ideal bond
being pursued in women's fiction and the chief difficulties which ob-
struct it. The Catherine/Heathcliff bond of *Wuthering Heights* provides a
mythic image of the double. The relationship between Catherine and
Heathcliff, prior to their co-optation by social forms, represents the double in pure form: an ideal image which, because of its defiance of gender, is innately antithetical to patriarchal culture. Charlotte Brontë
shares a similar focus in *Jane Eyre*, though within a different context. The
Jane/Rochester bond of this novel serves both as reflection of and coun-
terpoint to the mythic ideal. Equally concerned with an image of male-
female relation that transcends social strictures of class and gender,
Charlotte Brontë also explores a male/female double but seeks to place
that bond within a social context. The result of such social placement is
inevitably a compromise, or a dilution, of the gender-transcendent
bond, since entering the social world always entails the conflicts of
sexual politics.

Most recent feminist readings of *Jane Eyre* have focused primarily
on the Jane/Bertha double of the novel as representing the female protagonist's (and, numerous critics suggest, the author's) ambivalence

about and resistance to the constraints of gender.[1] I believe the male/female double is also central to Brontë's text, however, and, far from conflicting with the body of theory on the female/female double, is complementary to it. The Jane/Bertha double helps explain why the model of relationship expressed by Jane and Rochester is pursued: because of the keen awareness of gender confinement Brontë and her protagonist reflect.

Charlotte and Emily Brontë's use of male pseudonyms, of course, reflects authorial awareness of such confinement. Publishing as Currer and Ellis Bell—their having, as Charlotte wrote in her preface to the 1847 edition of *Wuthering Heights,* "a sort of conscientious scruple at assuming Christian names positively masculine" (4)—suggests a desire to effect a certain gender-neutral stance by which fiction alone is what matters. The same purpose can be attributed to their attempt to create a neutral space for male-female bonding. In what sort of space can gender contraints be "neutralized" is the central question. And, if such a social space can be constructed, at what cost?

Let us look first at the dimensions of the male/female double as it exists in pure form, in nature, outside the social world. The milieu of Wuthering Heights and the Yorkshire moors is the geographical space this bond occupies, a space which is, to some extent, "apatriarchal" (to use Pratt's term). The tenants of Wuthering Heights share a relatively class-and gender-free environment. Servant and gentleman sit down to supper together; the gypsy foundling is raised as the gentleman's son; and the children, Catherine and Heathcliff, sleep, play, and dream together with no distinction by gender or class. Patriarchal legitimacy is subverted from the start. With the entrance of Heathcliff, ordinary rules of father-son lineage and of class privilege are suspended. The gentleman names the foundling, the "devil's offspring," for his own dead son (the name itself signifying more a connection with nature than with culture), and the way is prepared for the antipatriarchal saga to begin. The relationship between Catherine and Heathcliff is the heart of this saga.

With her lost brother restored to her, Catherine is strengthened and empowered, as is Heathcliff by his new-found sister. Empowerment exists in connection; depletion in division. Patriarchal order continually threatens to impose division, however, and to sever their bond. The misery of separation is the theme of our first introduction to Catherine, of course, in the diary entries Lockwood discovers during his first sleepless night at the Heights. Catherine records her misery and anger at Hindley's insistence that she and Heathcliff sleep in separate beds. Not surprisingly, the time at which this separation occurs is puberty, and it is the result of the temporary restoration of patriarchal order effected by Hindley's marriage. The double bond between Catherine and Heathcliff is most pure in the asexual, apatriarchal, even atemporal world of child-hood and of nature. Catherine and Heathcliff do not even believe them-selves to be subject to social realities. Like all human beings, though—even those living on the geographical fringes of the world—they are sub-ject to social influence, and that influence demands male/female division.

On the eve of Catherine's "fall" into the social world of the Lintons, or more accurately, of her being "grabbed" by that world, as Gilbert and Gubar point out,[2] Catherine and Heathcliff get a glimpse of the sexual divisiveness which is characteristic of male/female relationships in the social world. After running off from the Heights, they station them-selves as spies outside the windows of the Lintons' Thrushcross Grange. Initially impressed by the Grange's elegance, they finally scoff at the "petted things" within, Edgar and Isabella in the midst of a quarrel over who is to have a pet dog. Heathcliff says to Nelly after-ward, "When would you catch me wishing to have what Catherine wanted? Or find us by ourselves . . . divided by the whole room" (65).

The contrast between the gender-transcendent bond of Catherine and Heathcliff on the outside, and that other brother-sister bond within, is most apparent here. What separate Edgar and Isabella are possessive-ness, jealousy, a struggle for power and privilege: familiar features of male/female relations in the grip of sexual politics. Catherine and Heathcliff, as mythic double, are not subject to such politics. There is no struggle for power between them because their connection tran-scends social rules and roles.

This indifference to social situations is surely the principal reason for Catherine's marriage to Linton. Since her bond to Heathcliff exists outside of social forms, Catherine sees no reason why her marriage to Linton should interfere with it. The one has nothing to do with the other. The intensity of Catherine's "double-feeling" is most evident in her oft-quoted exclamation, "I am Heathcliff" which, taken literally, explains perfectly why marriage between them is impossible. Marriage for him, as well as for herself, however, is not. It is, in fact, as if Cather-ine believed Linton would be marrying them both, enabling them to-gether to rise to a more comfortable and secure place in the world. Given Catherine's limited experience of society, her näiveté is entirely understandable. She has no comprehension of the rigidity of social forms for male/female relations and the extent to which her bond with Heathcliff is antithetical to them.

After their "fall" into social reality, Catherine and Heathcliff suc-cumb to the influence of gender and class, each seeming to retreat into his/her respective sex role. They appear, in fact, to effect a virtual parody of masculinity and femininity. Originally high-spirited and vital, Catherine, as wife of Linton, gradually weakens and becomes frail. Still willful, though trapped by the powerlessness of her feminine role, she resorts to the desperate tactics of the powerless: self-starvation, self-confinement, and eventual self-destruction. Separated from Heathcliff, she is also cut off from her strength. She is, in fact, "lost" to her true self as her later haunting of Lockwood at Wuthering Heights suggests, when she tells him she has been lost on the moors for twenty years.

The "mad scene" with Nelly, shortly before Catherine's death, offers striking evidence of her sense of fragmentation and self-loss. Catherine tells Nelly her dream of alienation from her present self, describing her sense that the past seven years (years of her marriage to Linton) were an utter blank between two scenes of separation from Heathcliff. The present grief is somehow wrenched out of context and melds with the prior one. She feels herself once again the young girl ordered to sleep apart from Heathcliff for the first time. Her sense of separation from herself is so intense that her own reflected image is alien to her; she does not recognize the self she has become. "Why am I so changed?" (132), she wails, staring at her image in the mirror. Catherine's true self, the one she recognizes and which gives her strength, is antithetical to marriage with the civilized Linton (or indeed to motherhood) and is intricately connected with Heathcliff. Separation from Heathcliff is separation from self.

"Post-lapsarian" Heathcliff is similarly fragmented. Like Catherine, who succumbs to the disempowering influences of femininity (and is thus alienated from self), Heathcliff emerges as a caricature of masculinity, bent on power and vengeance. He becomes ruthless and hard, seeking to acquire power over others at any cost. It is, of course, important to note that after their separation, Catherine and Heathcliff both (though separately) enter the realm of sexual politics. Together, their bond intact, they need have nothing to do with the power discrepancies of gender and class; they exist outside such characteristics of the social order. Separate, they must struggle to live within them. Given the social equation of masculinity with power, Heathcliff is not compelled to enter the trap of powerlessness which Catherine inhabits after her co-optation. The pursuit and exercise of power, in fact, become the center of his life. It is a power utterly cut off from any mediating, humanizing influence, separated even from a sense of purpose. Heathcliff becomes a parody of the patriarch. Although the dimensions and the implications of his entrapment are different from Catherine's (because of their different gender prescriptions), he is equally alienated from self and life. He is, in fact, lost to himself in the same way that Catherine is lost to herself.

It is Catherine's death which seals Heathcliff's fate of self-aliena-tion. His agonized cry to Catherine, "Oh, God! would you like to live with your soul in the grave?" (162), accurately foretells his future. More caricature than character, Heathcliff seems, after Catherine's death, to recede into the bleak, monotonous landscape of the moors he inhabits. He becomes similarly stolid, one-dimensional, and consistent; it is as pointless to seek answers, motives, or feelings in Heathcliff as it is in the unremitting terrain.

This is so, at least, until the "change" comes, when Heathcliff, apparently emulating Cathy's death, throws off all social, and even physical ties, reuniting with her in death. These scenes of transforma-tion, particularly those in which he articulates his experience to Nelly, significantly parallel Catherine's dying scenes (also with Nelly as un-comprehending audience).[3] Heathcliff, too, of course, abstains from food and rest, working himself up, as Catherine did, to a fever pitch of heightened sensitivity and awareness. At times it is almost as if Cather-ine herself is keeping Heathcliff from eating, through the supernatural bond she holds with him, as if she is compelling him along the path of her own death to join her beyond it.

During this period of maddened transformation, Heathcliff also ex-presses a sense of separateness from his physical form. He has almost "to remind himself to breathe and his heart to beat" (301), he says to Nelly. He takes none of his former interest in exerting power over oth-ers, growing indifferent to the developing relationship between Hareton and Catherine Linton, indifferent even to their existence. He tells Nelly that he sees Catherine everywhere, that even "my own features mock me with a resemblance" (301), a significant parallel to Catherine's earlier confusion over her mirrored image.

The Catherine/Heathcliff bond transcends the physical plane as fully as it does the social. If there is no appropriate social form for their interaction, there is also clearly no physical form. Their connection ap-pears to be too intense to accommodate the limitations of physical inter-action. The only scene of physical intimacy between Catherine and Heathcliff, after all, is the one which precedes Catherine's death, and it is striking in its intensity and violence. Catherine, with "white cheek" and "bloodless lip, " seizes Heathcliff's hair with such force she pulls it out by the roots, and Heathcliff's hold on her arm leaves blue bruises behind. Nelly feared her mistress would "never be released alive" from their embrace, and when she attempted to interfere, Heathcliff "gnashed" at her and "foamed like a mad dog." "I did not feel as if I were in the company of a creature of my own species" (161), Nelly says. Physical interaction is apparently inadequate as an expression of their bond.

The extent to which the social order is disrupted by the Catherine/ Heathcliff bond, from Heathcliff's arrival at Wuthering Heights and usurpation of the son's place until his death, suggests that the male/ female double cannot be socially placed. Patriarchal social forms demand divisions, between man and woman, between gentry and servant, between nature and culture. Through their bond, Catherine and Heathcliff deny these divisions, thus threatening their extinction. Nelly's relief and approval over the displacement of the first generation by the second can certainly be perceived (as Nelly's views always are) as society's breathing a sigh of relief at the end of a distressing era.

The comedic marriage of Hareton Earnshaw and Catherine Linton Heathcliff effects a restoration of patriarchal order—Catherine teaches Hareton to read his own name as patriarch over the door of the Heights, thus assisting in this reclamation of his rightful place as an Earnshaw— but it is a significantly qualified one. There is no gender-transcendent connection in the second generation bond; the restored social order forbids this possibility. Still, Catherine and Hareton maintain something of the first generation's spirit. Catherine Linton Heathcliff Earnshaw's very name, of course, suggests a combination of all three hereditary possibilities, the civilized and the savage in unlikely union. Catherine has inherited, too, a fair portion of her mother's willfulness and strength, as in her consistent fearlessness of Heathcliff and her tyrannical manner with Hareton. Hareton, too, in his identification with Heathcliff (Hareton being the only one genuinely to mourn Heathcliff's death) and his resemblance to Cathy, suggests a connection with the older generation which Nelly and her kind would undoubtedly disclaim.

The subversive threat of the Catherine/Heathcliff bond is, in fact, still alive in the second generation. Even Nelly, mouthpiece of conventional practicality that she is, is afraid to be out in the dark or in the house alone because of the ghost stories she has heard. Wuthering Heights is to be closed up, apparently too grim and ominous a place to inhabit. And on rainy nights, Catherine and Heathcliff are said to walk. Significantly, it is children, we are told, who most often see these ghosts, perhaps because, like Catherine and Heathcliff, children are freer of social rules and forms and are thus better able to perceive things those forms do not allow. Certainly there is abundant evidence to suggest that the subversive threat posed by the Catherine/Heathcliff bond still exists and may once again surface (if only in the imagination of the female writer) as active foil to patriarchy. The continuance of social order, it seems, necessitates a certain anxious watch on that possibility and an avoidance of its influence.

The narrative method of *Wuthering Heights* suggests that Emily Brontë had some awareness of the subversiveness of her fiction. Brontë masks her story behind veils of narrators: Lockwood, who has it from Ellen Dean, who has it occasionally even from others (Zillah, the Heights housekeeper, or Isabella Linton). This remarkably distanced narration leads one to ask, of course, why the subterfuge? An at least partial answer is that Emily Brontë, an individual of solitary habit and reserved, independent mind, was well aware of the likely nineteenth-century response to her antipatriarchal text and couched her tale accordingly, distancing herself from it as far as possible.[4] She may also have shared her readers' ambivalence: on the one hand, she may have embraced the asocial and amoral power of the characters and relationships she created, while, on the other, she may have recognized and sought to divorce herself from the very real subversiveness they embodied.

Whatever the motive of this narrative approach, what is certain is its effect. Without sacrificing realistic depiction of her characters and the Yorkshire setting they inhabit, Brontë lent her fiction the tone and atmosphere of myth. The method by which it comes to us, through one narrator then another, suggests an oral storytelling mode and creates a sense, not of the story having been constructed for us, but of its having been handed down to us, as something which exists on its own and which has existed for a very long time. This mythic tone is part of the reason, I think, why the image of cross-gender relationship epitomized by Catherine and Heathcliff has recurred so often in the fictions of women authors.

Emily Brontë did not, perhaps could not, construct a social context which would accommodate the type of male/female bond she created in *Wuthering Heights.* And perhaps there is none. Such a bond is decidedly hostile to traditional social order. Its iconoclastic energy requires placement in the mythic world, above and beyond the restrictions of gender and class, to an extent, even of time and space. Brontë's temperament and perspective, of course, lent itself to this approach. Unlike her sister, Emily Brontë was most comfortable in isolation from society, most at home in the secluded Haworth parsonage on the Yorkshire moors. Her few attempts to enter into society (like her stay with Charlotte at the French academy in Brussels) ended dismally; she became ill, lonely, and homesick.[5] For Emily Brontë, the social world was not the soil in which to grow the dynamic potential of individual creativity, or of dynamic relationships. It was, in fact, a foil to the dynamic life. So it is in her fiction. The mythic image of male/female interaction she describes in *Wuthering Heights,* however, haunts the fictions of many women writers, both those which share her mythic context and those which do not.

Certainly her sister shared an interest in this image. Since we know that Charlotte Brontë had the opportunity to read *Wuthering Heights* before writing *Jane Eyre,*[6] it is tempting to theorize about the effect this reading had on her own choice of subject. At the center of each novel is a male/female double, a gender and class-transcendent relationship, which defies social norms. Although their focus is similar, the context in which it is situated is quite different. Charlotte Brontë places her double much more decisively within a social context. The relationship between Jane Eyre and Edward Fairfax Rochester is very much a socially placed one, with clear delineation of class and of sexual and economic roles. Brontë's task in *Jane Eyre* is to fit the male/female bond into traditional social structure (i.e. marriage) without destroying it; in other words, to make social institutions accommodate that bond.

Social placement of the gender-transcendent bond is no easy task. Inevitably it involves conflicts—conflicts which emerge from the divisions of gender and class which society imposes on all individuals. Jane Eyre's awareness of these divisions and the restrictions they impose on her has been dealt with in sufficient detail to preclude doing so here.[7] It bears repeating, however, that the central purpose of the early sections of the novel (the Gateshead and Lowood sequences) is to show Jane developing a keen awareness of social divisions: the oppressiveness of class privilege (from John Reed who instructs her in her "dependent" status), of hypocritical religious dogma as fashioned by the rich for the poor (from Mr. Brocklehurst), and of the gender-defined code of self-sacrifice and passivity which society esteems for women, encountered in such models as Helen Burns and Miss Temple. This early instruction in social forms, and her place as female within them, fosters in Jane an independent mind, capable of viewing the world with a critical eye because of her habitual position as outsider. Having experienced the constraints of gender and class, she cannot be content with a traditional bond which enforces them; having lived as the socially disenfranchised, she is capable of defying custom. This social training prepares the way for the egalitarian bond Jane attempts to form with Rochester.

It is important to note the very different character of this double as compared to that of *Wuthering Heights;* even the terms of our discussion are altered. Instead of the ideal union of the double on the mythic plane, we speak of an egalitarian relationship, the change in vocabulary reflecting the change in context. In the mythic world, the concept of equality is irrelevant. Being asocial and apatriarchal, the mythic double is also apolitical. Since there are no political divisions, there are no political conflicts, hence no need for words to describe them. The social context of *Jane Eyre* necessitates such language, and the relationship between Jane and Rochester necessarily involves the political conflicts this language reflects.

Interestingly, Jane and Rochester's first meeting, on the road to Millcote, presents an image of connection momentarily free from such conflicts, and it prefigures the way in which their bond will ultimately challenge gender and class roles. Brontë places this first interaction outside the social milieu, away even from the smaller social world of Thornfield. Jane and Rochester are, initially, unaware of each other's social and economic status, thus temporarily free from the forms of behavior and interaction attendant on those roles. The exchange is a brief one. Rochester, injured in a fall from his horse, is compelled to lean on Jane for support, and Jane, contrary to feminine custom, insists upon helping him. The scene prefigures significantly the way in which their bond will defy conventional roles and rules of interaction as it develops.

Equally suggestive is the folkloric atmosphere in which Brontë envelops this meeting. As Jane waits for Rochester's horse to appear through the dusk, she recalls tales of the Gytrash (a hostile animal spirit which accosts solitary travelers) which she was told as a child. She half expects Rochester's dog, Pilot, as it approaches her by the road, to stare into her face with "strange pretercanine eyes" (144), thus, according to legend, prophesying the death of someone near. Rochester says of this experience later that when Jane came into view he "thought unaccountably of fairy tales" and that he'd half a mind to demand whether she'd "bewitched his horse" (153). Imbuing this first meeting with elements of fantasy and folklore suggests a connection with the mythic bond of Catherine and Heathcliff, as if this bond too emerges from a kind of natural, apatriarchal space and shares some of the prepatriarchal, mythic potential associated with it.

Despite this somewhat mythic initiation, however, the development of Jane and Rochester's relationship is characterized largely by conflict. From their first conversation in the library at Thornfield, the terms of the conflict are clear. Rochester, in his typically gruff and "masterial" manner, asks if he may not assume a certain superiority based upon his age and worldly experience. Jane, habitually frank, responds, "Your claim to superiority depends on the use you have made of your time and experience" (165), thus putting her finger on Rochester's central problem. Rochester, we ultimately learn, has not made very effective use of the experience he boasts of here, and the use he has made of it poses a serious obstacle to the bond he desires with Jane. It is appar-

ent, from these early discussions, that the development of this relationship centers on a kind of testing of the boundaries of sexual and economic roles which inhibit the bond of equality they desire and a struggle
to cross them.

Both Jane and Rochester approach this conflict with ambivalence.
Although each is clearly drawn to the potential for equality they see
represented in the character and behavior of the other, neither is wholly
prepared to accept it. Thus their conflict is not only with the external
social forms of class and gender relations, but also with the internaliza-
tion of these forms as it affects their view of self and other. Jane experiences difficulty, for instance, in relinquishing her concept of self as
"dependent" (a self-image brutally enforced by her earlier experiences
at Gateshead and Lowood), and therefore has difficulty in seeing herself
as a suitable mate for Rochester. Through his feigned courtship of
Blanche Ingram (one much better suited to him socially), Rochester in
fact goads Jane into a declaration of her equality with him, into an
acknowledgement that "though rank and wealth sever us widely, I have
something in my brain and heart, in my blood and nerves, that assimi-
lates me mentally to him" (204). She struggles to suppress these feelings
of "assimilation," even imposing on herself the penance of drawing the
beautiful Blanche's portrait and comparing it with her own reflection
each morning.

Yet the bond continues to assert itself. The scene in which Rochester poses as a gypsy fortune-teller makes clear both the bond they feel
and the extent to which Rochester is manipulating Jane to acknowledge
it.[8] Disguised as an old gypsy-woman, Rochester pretends to tell Jane's
fortune, in so doing demonstrating remarkable insight into her character, even to anticipating his own rejection. He interprets Jane's brow as
saying "I have an inward treasure born with me, which can keep me
alive if all extraneous delights should be withheld, or offered only at a
price I cannot afford to give" (230). Jane is so transfixed by the accuracy
of the old woman's foretelling that she enters a kind of trance and
awakens from it echoing Keats' query "Did I wake or sleep? Had I been
dreaming?" (231). Before Rochester takes off his disguise, Jane experiences a sense of blended identities which strongly reflects the double-
bond she has been striving to deny. The old woman's voice, her accent,
gesture and all, Jane says, suddenly "were familiar to me as my own
face in a glass—as the speech of my own tongue" (231). Soon after, Jane
recognizes her "master's" hand and "the play is played out."

Though Jane is not here forced to a declaration of love, the intensity
of their bond is strongly impressed upon her, urging her toward that
acknowledgment. The larger masquerade of Rochester's intended mar-

riage to Miss Ingram is played out when Jane, in anger and sorrow at her supposed removal to Ireland, finally declares her equality with Rochester, exclaiming, "Do you think, because I am poor, obscure, plain, and little, I am soulless and heartless. . . . I am not talking to you now through the medium of custom, conventionalities, nor even of mortal flesh: it is my spirit that addresses your spirit; just as if both had passed through the grave, and we stood at God's feet, equal—as we are!" "As we are!" repeats Mr. Rochester, "so, Jane!" (281). Custom and convention are put aside, their equality is acknowledged, and the idyllic courtship period ensues. Yet it, too, is defined by conflict. More than spiritual equality must be affirmed; a very real social equality must be achieved.

The brief courtship period, followed by the discovery of Bertha Mason, makes clear the economic and sexual/political conflicts which stand in the way. Jane is troubled by her "unworthiness," in social terms, to marry Rochester, as in her concern over Mrs. Fairfax's reaction which is, predictably, that "gentlemen in his station are not accustomed to marrying their governesses" (294). Rochester sets out, in an apparent attempt to put a superficial gloss of conventionality over their unconventional bond, to bedeck Jane with satins and jewels, which she finds annoying and degrading. Throughout the courtship, Jane resists Rochester's idolatry of her, rightly seeing it as a misrepresentation both of her reality and of the reality of their bond. Jane insists on remaining herself, continuing as Adele's governess and resisting Rochester's romantic projections. Though drawn to her independence and uniqueness, Rochester is yet unable to accept her as such, striving instead, once he has secured her love, to mold her into the appropriate social form for a man in his "station," and to exert his dominance by attaching her to him like his watch-guard (299).

These conflicts, of course, culminate in the discovery of Bertha Mason and the aborted wedding, and they play a significant part in Jane's subsequent flight from Thornfield. Jane rejects Rochester not merely because of convention, but because she begins to distrust his love. That distrust is based on his treatment of Bertha (for whom Jane feels sympathy), as well as on his use of women since his marriage to Bertha. Jane fears, if she goes with him to the south of France, that she will in time become another of his "inferior" mistresses (like Celine Varens) whom he will also come to regard with disdain.

Bertha Mason, the evil secret hidden in Rochester's house, reflects the secret hidden in his psyche:[9] that he has not acknowledged his own complicity, both in his false marriage and in the events of his adult life since then. Perceiving himself as sole victim he has victimized others, as if by right. These habits of mind have been fostered by his social situation as privileged upper-class male. Thus the internalized influences of gender and class prevent Rochester from attaining what he most wants. Bertha Mason's existence, not only as wife, but also as symbol of Rochester's inability to meet Jane as an equal, represents a serious impediment to the bond both Jane and Rochester desire. Before that bond is possible for Rochester, he must exorcise that part of himself symbolized by Bertha, which he ultimately does via the "purification by fire" of Thornfield's destruction. Upon reaching out to Bertha, acknowledging their connection, the need for both secret and prison-house is eradicated, and he is free to engage with Jane on a level of equality.

Jane, too, must undergo certain psychic preparation. The egalitarian bond demands independence of both members, psychic as well as social, and the sequence of events which follows Jane's flight from Thornfield assists her in securing this. She flees the emotional threat to her independence posed by Rochester only to face another one, again in the shape of male domination: the psychological threat of St. John Rivers.

For Jane, a significant impediment to egalitarian male/female bonding (and the female independence it demands) is the feminine propensity for self-sacrifice and self-denial which was fostered by her social experience, and which Gilligan discusses as psychologically the most dangerous effect of women's training in empathy and responsibility to others. The clearly masochistic three-day journey Jane undertakes after separation from Rochester, by evil coincidence leaving behind her money and possessions (thus virtually starving), reveals her tendency toward martyrdom, which St. John capitalizes upon fully.

If Rochester utilized certain emotional manipulations to attain his end (marriage to Jane), St. John exercises psychological ones. He exerts tremendous power over Jane, rendering her progressively weaker, more confused, and more submissive. Whereas Rochester presumably offered Jane the spirit of marriage without the form, St. John wants the form without the spirit, desiring her only as "helpmate" on his missionary quest to India. Jane wants both: the social form of marriage infused with a spirit of love and equality. She disdains St. John's conception of marriage because it is a denial of the bond she seeks, rightly perceiving that compliance with St. John's desires means "disowning half her nature" (424). Yet she is severely threatened by the psychological sway he holds over her, a power she has given him because of the feminine code of passivity and self-sacrifice she has internalized.

Jane is seemingly rescued from St. John's influence by the re-emergence of her bond with Rochester. She hears Rochester's voice calling to her in the garden of Moor House, a voice which she says comes also from "inside" herself. Rochester says later of this telepathic moment that "In spirit, I believe, we must have met" (472). As their bond emerged from a supernatural, mythic beginning, so finally it is cemented. Jane's triumph over the spirit of female martyrdom has prepared her for the bond with Rochester she now moves to secure.

The inheritance Jane receives from her uncle John Eyre in Madeira also contributes significantly to her ability to rejoin Rochester on a basis of equality. "I am an independent woman now," Jane tells Rochester when they meet at Ferndean, and she means by this not only psychological independence (though she has this, too), but a very real economic independence.[10] The tangible social equality afforded by this legacy frees Jane forever from her "dependent" social status and is an important preliminary to the egalitarian bond she and Rochester establish.

The final image of Jane and Rochester's marriage is an idyllic one, of "perfect concord" in all things. Rochester's experience in the destruction of Thornfield and the injuries he received have rendered him more cognizant of his own responsibility in the events of his life and considerably less "masterial" with others. He is more willing to lean on the arm Jane offered him at their first meeting, more able now to regard her as an equal. For her part, Jane says, "I love you better now, when I can really be useful to you, than I did in your state of proud independence, when you disdained every part but that of the giver and protector" (470).

The level of their interaction, as Jane describes it ten years after her marriage, reflects strongly the kind of blended identities and consciousness-sharing which I associate with the male/female double. They know no weariness of each other's society, Jane says, "any more than we each do of the pulsation of the heart that beats in our separate bosoms. . . . To talk to each other is but a more animated and an audible thinking" (476).

Equality on every level—of spirit, of psyche, and of pocket—is necessary for the double-bond to be sustained in the social world. All the socially imposed divisions of gender and class must be transcended, both in their external and internalized forms. Brontë strives to convince, I believe, that all this has been achieved. Yet the enormity of the task has exacted a heavy price, and the idyllic marriage clearly has its limitations. The geographical space it inhabits is, after all, just barely "social." Ferndean is off the beaten track, buried in woods, and always considered an unhealthful place. (Rochester deemed it an inhumane environment even for Bertha.) And their life together there is generally a solitary one, relieved only by annual visits with Diana and Mary Rivers.

One is led to ask why this isolation is necessary. A partial answer, I think, lies in the difficulties which social placement of the male/female double involves. Charlotte Brontë's *Jane Eyre* makes abundantly clear the concrete ways in which social forms conflict with male/female bonding. Emily Brontë's novel suggests that the male/female bond, in its purest form, is in fact antithetical to social forms. Society insists upon divisions, between man and woman, between wealthy and poor, between self and other. To form and sustain a gender-transcendent bond in the social sphere, it is necessary to challenge this equation and to replace conflict with cooperation, division with connection.

Wuthering Heights and *Jane Eyre* represent alternative (though often overlapping) contexts in which this shared interest is explored: an image of male/female bonding which defies the constraints of culture. These fictions make clear both the ideal image of transcended divisions and the extent to which such bonds challenge social norms and structures. The "cord of communion" (280) which Rochester feels connecting himself and Jane, in other words, defies the cultural divisions which influence our definitions of self and other.

The concrete obstacles which emerge when this image is situated within social forms are as much a reality in the fictions of modern women writers as in those of the Brontës. Although over eighty years intervene between Charlotte Brontë's representation of the sexual/political conflicts which occur when a man and a woman attempt to connect across the boundaries of gender and class, and Virginia Woolf's fictional explorations on this theme, the reality is very much the same. Modern awareness of gender has, if anything, delineated the problem more clearly: gender divides, in deeply entrenched ways. The modern fictions I examine seem to suggest that those seeking a way to transcend gender must find a way to subvert social influence; to effect a compromise which, though perhaps diluting the bond, still allows it to exist (as perhaps in *Jane Eyre*); or to abandon the social sphere altogether.

Psychic Bonding in *Mrs. Dalloway*

I hate the power of life to divide.

The Diary of Virginia Woolf

Perhaps no twentieth-century writer has defined more clearly what divides men and women, or has been more concerned with transcending such divisions, than Virginia Woolf. Though she examined the possibilities for male/female bonds in a variety of contexts (romantic and otherwise), Woolf held consistently to a perception of masculinity and femininity as essentially distinct and, to varying degrees, opposed. *A Room of One's Own* (1929) marks the culmination and the most succinct expression of this awareness. She articulates here clear differences in male/female ways of seeing, ordering, and representing reality: "it is obvious that the values of women differ very often from the values which have been made by the other sex" (76–77), she asserts; and, since "these values are inevitably transferred from life to fiction" (77), the "creative power" of women "differs greatly from the creative power of men" (91).

The aesthetic context of Woolf's discussion of gender division is more than apparent. Because of Woolf's concept of androgyny, however, *A Room of One's Own* has often been misinterpreted as positing some ideal form for male/female interaction.[1] The fact is, however, that the sight of two people getting into a taxi, that image which sparked Woolf's androgynous theory, and which she said "seems to ease the mind of some strain" (100), means precisely what it says: it is an image of the mind, the "creative mind," Woolf clarifies, and is by no means intended as a model for the social interaction of men and women. Woolf makes this most explicit: "Some collaboration has to take place in the mind between the woman and the man before the act of creation can be accomplished. Some marriage of opposites has to be consummated" (108). Clearly, Woolf's concept of androgyny (like Coleridge's before her) is intended as an aesthetic image only; as an image of male/female bonding in daily life, she is clearly aware of its limitations. It is, in fact, only on the level of consciousness that transcendence of gender constraints is possible. Woolf's phrase for the androgynous mind as a "marriage of opposites" makes clear her firm sense of masculinity and femininity as innately different.

From her tentative explorations of romantic bonding in the early fictions through the development of her aesthetic image of androgyny in *A Room of One's Own*, Woolf tests the boundaries of gender and develops a clear understanding of its power to divide. Rachel Vinrace's cry of frustration in *The Voyage Out*, "It's no good; we should live separate; we cannot understand each other" (156), is a succinct recognition of that schism between masculine and feminine perception. The development of Rachel and Terence Hewet's romantic interaction is one of recurrent failed attempts to connect, which draw an increasingly frustrated sense of separateness in their wake. Their engagement having originated in the mythical region of the Amazon, in apatriarchal space, if you will, Rachel and Terence are unable to sustain it against the divisive impositions of society. And while Terence claims that finally, at Rachel's death, they achieve the union which eluded them in life, the nightmare images of Rachel's fatal illness are more suggestive of a desperate retreat by a threatened self than of communion.

Night and Day, despite its more comic tone, presents a similarly dismal picture of the possibilities for real understanding between men and women. The illusory quality of romance becomes even more a central concern here, from Ralph Denham's initial falling in love with Katharine Hilbery for her way of pouring tea, through the romantic mania both experience as the relationship intensifies. Thus, in both investigating and satirizing the romantic impulse it describes, *Night and Day* might best be described as a romantic parody. Though the novel ends on a note of union, of order, and of approbation for the "enchanted region" of romance Katharine and Ralph inhabit, it is also a "difficult region" in which "together they groped" (506). They continue to struggle with their "lapses" (473): Ralph's "lapse" into romanticized projection of Katharine after which he fears "he only loved her shadow and cared nothing for her reality" (473); Katharine's—as a response to Ralph's—into detached self-absorption "which carried her away with such intensity that she sharply resented any recall to her companion's side" (473). Katharine's "lapse" into detachment is, of course, markedly similar to Rachel Vinrace's state of mind and shares similar motives: a voyage inward to escape imposition from without.[2]

The writing of *Night and Day*, useful to Woolf stylistically as an exercise in "realistic fiction," also crystallized her perception of the inadequacy of romantic bonding as a means of transcending the divisions of gender. Romance, in effect, requires division, even distortion, and thus infringement upon the reality of the self. Though its aim is union, its method requires separation. In such explorations of male-female relations in her early fictions, Woolf makes clear the reality of gender division which underlies the aesthetic image of "communion" she is moving toward.

Of all the writers whose fictions I am examining, Woolf makes most explicit the essential difficulties of male/female bonding and the distinctive character of the male/female double of women's fiction. The problem, simply, is that because of the impact of gender (and its attendant differences in experience and outlook), there is an intractable barrier between men and women which inhibits bonding. As a general rule, cross-gender connection involves the subordination of one self to the other, and since, as Woolf notes, it is "masculine values which prevail" (77), it is most often the female self to be subordinated. Rachel Vinrace and Katharine Hilbery are reflections of such female selfhood threatened by the impositions of romantic bonding.

The project, then, is a complex one: to achieve a male/female connection which transcends the divisions imposed by gender while sustaining the separateness and integrity of the self. It is in *Mrs. Dalloway* that this project is most directly and successfully pursued. Clarissa's and Septimus's insistence on "privacy of the soul," combined with their unique consciousness sharing, represents Woolf's best solution to the dilemma of gender division (one which she eventually carries even further in *The Waves*).

In relation to the mythic-social context suggested by the Brontës' fictions, Woolf's fiction seems to occupy a tenuous middle ground between the two. In its suggestion that true male/female bonding is not workable within the social contexts of marriage, romantic bonding, or ordinary daily interaction, it appears most aligned with Emily Brontë's approach. Woolf herself thought "Emily was a greater poet than Charlotte," primarily because of what she labeled Charlotte's "constricted" and "self-centred" assertions: "I love," "I hate," "I suffer." It is the absence of the "I" in *Wuthering Heights* that Woolf, with her abhorrence of egotism, most admired. She believed, because of this "I-focus," that Charlotte Brontë "does not attempt to solve the problems of human life," that "she is even unaware that such problems exist" (*Common Reader*, 161). It is clear, however, that Brontë was interested in human problems—such as the problem of gender division—and that Woolf shared this interest. Woolf's unique project in *Mrs. Dalloway* was to show male/female connection within a social context—post-war England—but without the social forms which restrict male/female bonding. The means by which Woolf reconciled these two divergent tasks—both transcending and situating within social forms—was to extend the psychological dimension of her fiction and to invent an aesthetic form which would unify the opposing principles she sought to connect.

The development of her "stream of consciousness" technique for the unfolding of character and the revealing of relationships between characters provided Woolf the psychological depth she was seeking and an aesthetic form flexible enough to contain it. In a diary note on *Mrs. Dalloway*, Woolf notes her "discovery": "How I dig out beautiful caves behind my characters: I think that gives exactly what I want; humanity, humour, depth. The idea is that the caves shall connect and each comes to daylight at the present moment" (*Writer's Diary*, 59). This "caving" metaphor perfectly captures the kind of subterranean excavation of character we find in *Mrs. Dalloway* and describes well the method she discovered to transcend the divisions posed by gender, as well as by ego. In a similar vein is Woolf's note about her "prime discovery so far," her "tunneling process, by which I tell the past by installments, as I have need of it" (60). Like the previous discovery, this marked a significant increase in momentum during the writing of *Mrs. Dalloway*. Beneath the surface of social interaction, even of personality, these techniques are a significant part of the aesthetics Woolf was developing to transcend division. As her "beautiful caves" explore beneath the surface of characters and reveal the deeper connections between them, so her "tunneling process" reconciles the opposition of past and present. For Woolf, transcendence of gender division (and of virtually all divisions) occurs—if I may extend her metaphor once more—underground, in not the conscious, but the unconscious mind,[4] in the fullness and complexity of the self which defies categorization.

Woolf said of *Mrs. Dalloway* that she had "almost too many ideas for it. I want to give life and death, sanity and insanity . . . to criticize the social system" (*Writer's Diary*, 56). Elsewhere she says she feels as if she could "use up everything I've ever thought" (60). The dimensions of experience made available to her by these aesthetic "discoveries" must indeed have been exhilarating. The primary vehicle, however, for the expression (and unification) of opposites Woolf alludes to in her diary (and the attendant breadth of perspective this entails) is the doubling of Clarissa Dalloway and Septimus Warren Smith. On October 16, 1922, Woolf writes in her working notebook: "Suppose it to be connected this way: Sanity and insanity. Mrs. D. seeing the truth. SS seeing the insane truth. The pace to be given by the gradual increase of S's insanity on the one side; by the approach of the party on the other."[5] That the very structure of the novel, as well as its thematic concern with revealing and uniting alternate states of being, hinges upon the Clarissa/Septimus double is apparent from this notation.

Their reciprocal, shared identity is made equally explicit by Woolf's statement in the introduction to the Modern Library edition of *Mrs. Dalloway* (1928) that "in the first version Septimus, who later is intended to be her double, had no existence; and that Mrs. Dalloway was originally to kill herself, or perhaps merely to die at the end of the party" (vi). The alternate, but intensely shared, realities of Septimus and Clarissa effect the transcendence of gender division Woolf was seeking, and, because they have no social interaction whatever, perfect integrity of self is sustained. This transcendence of barriers allows for the intensity and breadth of experience Woolf describes with such enthusiasm in her diary, and for the unification of opposing principles she sought.

Though Clarissa and Septimus do not interact, they are consistently linked via images and events which fix them first in place and time, and then in sensibility, by virtue of their similar responses. What is revealed is an intimate sharing of consciousness which transcends not only the division of gender, but also of social position, of experience, and finally even of death.

The initial linking image which introduces us to Septimus and begins the pattern of psychological connection with Clarissa, is that of the prime minister's car which passes down Bond Street, drawing a wake of awe, respect, and patriotic zeal behind it, however ignorant passersby are of the car's inhabitant. Like the skywriting aeroplane which follows it, like the sounding of Big Ben, the car is a unifying focal point, not only for Septimus and Clarissa, but for everyone, regardless of gender, class, or place. It momentarily imposes order and generates a shared sensibility which transcends social boundaries. Clarissa and Septimus are a part of this general coming-together but are also particularized as sharing a similar perspective. Clarissa reflects on the party she will give that night as a part of that magnificence, that "lustre" of "candelabras, glittering stars, breasts stiff with oak leaves" the car symbolizes. "She stiffened a little: so she would stand at the top of her stairs" (20). She feels herself a part of that semblance of order, coherence, and dignity the car suggests and sees her party as sharing the same important purpose.

Septimus Warren Smith, twenty years younger than Clarissa but similarly "beak-nosed" and intensely alert to his environment, sees on the dove-grey blind in the car window a "pattern like a tree" and a "gradual drawing together of everything to one centre before his eyes" (18). Like Clarissa, Septimus perceives a pattern of order and himself as an integral part of it, "rooted to the pavement, for a purpose"; but his madness separates him from the sense of affiliation Clarissa achieves with her parties. Clarissa's primary means of creating order are, of course, her parties. As Septimus perceives patterns like trees which order reality, drawing it all together toward one centre, so Clarissa "[sums] it all up in the moment" (192) at her party, drawing together, "like water round the piers of a bridge" (182), all the disparate individuals she invites. Clarissa and Septimus's responses to this first event make clear from the outset both their shared sensibility and their crucial difference. Although their ways of seeing the world are similar, their responses differ: Clarissa's giving her a way of coping, a sense of meaning; Septimus's leaving him only isolated and vulnerable.

Clarissa and Septimus's shared aesthetic sense of pattern-making, of creating or desiring to create order and wholeness out of apparent disunity, emerges for both from a sense of the precariousness of life and the malleability of selfhood. In his madness, Septimus sees himself everywhere, connected with the living as with the dead, with the trees, rocks, and birds equally with human beings. He perceives his role as to "[interpret] to mankind" (76) this tremendous pattern of connection; to "be scientific, above all scientific" (26); and to inform the prime minister: "the trees are alive," "there is no crime," "love, universal love" (75).

Septimus's vision of the elm trees in Regent's Park describes perfectly this pattern of universal order he perceives:

> But they beckoned; leaves were alive; trees were alive. And the leaves being connected by millions of fibres with his own body, there on the seat, fanned it up and down; when the branch stretched he, too, made that statement. . . . Sounds made harmonies with premeditation; the spaces between them were as significant as the sounds. A child cried. Rightly far away a horn sounded. All taken together meant the birth of a new religion. (26)

In Septimus's psychotic vision, nothing is detached or separated from anything else; all is part of a "premeditated" and harmonious whole; and Septimus's sense of his own identity is intricately connected with everything and everyone else.

Markedly similar, of course, is Clarissa's sense of "being laid out like a mist between the people she knew best, who lifted her on their branches as she had seen the trees lift the mist" (12). Her "transcendental theory" (169) is another expression of this shared perception of the diffuseness of self. It was meant, Peter Walsh tells us, "to explain the feeling they had of dissatisfaction; not knowing people; not being known. . . . It was unsatisfactory, they agreed, how little one knew people" (168). Thus Clarissa's theory is an attempt to transcend the restrictiveness of ego boundaries which separate self and other. On the bus going up Shaftesbury Avenue, Clarissa explains to Peter that,

> she felt herself everywhere; not "here, here, here"; and she tapped the back of the seat; but everywhere. . . . Odd affinities she had with people she had never spoken to, some woman in the street, some man behind a counter—even trees, or barns. It ended in a transcendental theory which, with her horror of death, allowed her to believe . . . that since our apparitions . . . are so momentary compared with the other, the unseen part of us, which spreads wide, the unseen might survive, be recovered somehow attached to this person or that, or even haunting certain places, after death. (169)

Septimus's and Clarissa's sense of a diffuse, extended self is of a kind, both in expression and in motivation; both are prompted by the desire to transcend divisions and to create a coherent, orderly world out of apparent chaos.

That such pattern-making is of crucial importance to each is reflected by their shared perception of the peril of daily life. Clarissa "always had the feeling that it was very, very dangerous to live even one day" (11); and Septimus, surrounded by the nightmare images of madness, the dead coming to life, a "dog turning into a man," has often the feeling that "the world has raised its whip; where will it descend?" (17).

The nearness of death is suggested repeatedly. The reader's perception of both Septimus and Clarissa is of individuals living very much on the edge. As Woolf's comments on her intended first version of the novel suggest, death is never far from Clarissa. Her physical vulnerability is made explicit: "her heart, affected, they said, by influenza," her having "grown very white since her illness" (6). Clarissa's repetition of the line from Shakespeare's *Cymbeline*, "fear no more the heat of the sun," which is echoed by Septimus just prior to his suicide, suggests a kind of psychological preparedness for death, as do her frequent musings on death's meaning: "did it matter that she must inevitably cease completely; all this must go on without her; did she resent it; or did it not become consoling to believe that death ended absolutely?" (11). Peter's spontaneous image of Clarissa's death, after the sounding of St. Margaret's with which he associates her, of "Clarissa falling where she stood, in her drawing-room" (56), suggests even more acutely the fragility of her life. These numerous foreshadowings of Clarissa's death, when it is ultimately Septimus's death we are given, suggests strongly the intensity of their psychological connection and the near interchangeability of their fates.

A significant parallel between Clarissa and Septimus which deserves comment is the relative amorphousness of their sexual orientation and the similar character of their marriages. Clarissa says she lacked "something central . . . something warm which broke up surfaces and rippled the cold contact of man and woman" (36), and she accepts that "narrower and narrower would her bed be" (35). Falling in love with women, however, is something "she could dimly perceive" (36) and had, in fact, experienced with Sally Seton as a girl. "The strange thing, on looking back," she says, "was the purity, the integrity, of her feeling for Sally. It was not like one's feeling for a man" (39). It was "completely disinterested," she comments, that is, utterly free of the dynamics of power and the risk of self-loss which tend to characterize romantic bonds between men and women. Clarissa's marriage with Richard, though having none of the passion of her relationship with Sally—or with Peter—does not threaten that integrity of self, that "virginity . . . which clung to her like a sheet" (36). Her marriage, in fact, provides a stable "foundation" for her life.

Septimus's marriage to Rezia is similarly lacking in sexual passion and similarly motivated by a need for a sustaining presence which does not threaten the self. By far the deeper bond, for Septimus, was that with his officer and friend, Evans. "It was a case of two dogs playing on a hearth-rug. . . . They had to be together, share with each other, fight with each other, quarrel with each other" (96). It is the death of Evans and Septimus's growing panic "that he could not feel" (96) which precipitate his madness and compel him to marry Rezia.

In light of the psychic connection between Septimus and Clarissa, this parallel fluidity of sexual attraction and affiliation raises some interesting questions about Woolf's conception of the relationship between sexuality and gender. One might reasonably conclude, given the inextricable interconnection of sexuality and gender, that transcendence of one leads to—and perhaps requires—transcendence of the other. As a prerequisite, in other words, to the psychological connection between Septimus and Clarissa across the boundary of gender, both must be shown to have traversed, at least tentatively, the boundary of heterosexuality. In a broader context, this parallel suggests that transcendence of one division in human life extends easily, and even necessarily, to another: crossing the boundary of sexuality leads to that of another, gender, and of another, ego. The implication is that one dimension of experience cannot be neatly separated from another; once one pulls the thread which loosely closes the seam between this and that dimension of human experience, the whole fabric may unravel, revealing the fact that the fabric is all the same, the placement of seams and separations an entirely arbitrary matter.

As Septimus and Clarissa's choice of marriage partners suggests, one of the most significant psychological parallels between them is their keen awareness of, and instinctive recoil from, the intrusiveness of "converters," or of "human nature" in Septimus's lexicon (Holmes, Bradshaw, Kilman, et al). Survival of the self depends not only upon establishing order and meaning (i.e., their shared aesthetic quest), but also upon maintaining that "privacy of the soul" (140) Clarissa requires. "Love and religion," intended as nurture and solace for the soul, Clarissa calls "the cruellest things in the world" (180), seeing them "clumsy, hot, domineering, hypocritical, eavesdropping, jealous, infinitely cruel and unscrupulous, dressed in a mackintosh coat, on the landing" (140). Meant to unite, love and religion in fact divide; instead of preserving and sustaining the self, they in fact assault it.

Preserving the integrity of her self is the most important aspect of Clarissa's character (as it is finally the primary reason for Septimus's suicide). It is the cause of Clarissa's rejection of Peter Walsh: "For in marriage a little licence, a little independence there must be between people living together day in and day out in the same house; which Richard gave her, and she him," whereas with Peter, "everything had to be shared; everything gone into" (10). Though the intensity of their bond is obvious—Peter says "she had influenced him more than any person he had ever known" (169); Clarissa feels that they "lived in each other" (11)—it is unworkable in daily life because it threatens the integrity of the self. Her decision is not without ambivalence, however. After their brief, emotional scene together, Clarissa thinks to herself, "this gaiety would have been mine all day" (52). She knows what she has sacrificed, but her choice is determined by personal necessity.

The bond between Peter and Clarissa, in fact, makes clear the limitations of androgyny as a model for male-female interaction, of which Woolf was well aware. Interestingly, the only scene which shows Clarissa and Peter alone together—when he visits in the afternoon to find her stitching her dress—is strikingly reminiscent of that scene Woolf includes in *A Room of One's Own* to describe the "renewal of creative power" which so many "illustrious men" have received from women: "He would open the door of drawing-room or nursery, I thought, and find her among her children perhaps, or with a piece of embroidery on her knee—at any rate, the centre of some different order and system of life, and the contrast between this world and his own . . .

would at once refresh and invigorate" (90). Like that of Rochester and Jane, Peter and Clarissa's relationship is one very clearly defined by gender division and sexual politics. As the preceding quote suggests, the most that can be hoped for from such a bond is a kind of harmonious sexual complementarity (i.e. androgyny) which severely restricts development and expression in gender-prescribed ways. Unlike Brontë, however, Woolf suggests no possibility of their being able to transcend this dynamic. Peter and Clarissa, however intense their interaction, are trapped by the constraints of gender, and it is these constraints which Clarissa perceives as oppressive.

Clarissa's reflections on the old lady who lives across the way perfectly represent her sense of the importance of distance between one and another for integrity of self. Like Septimus's vision of the trees, Clarissa's thoughts about the old woman going from room to room, while Big Ben tolls, have almost a sacred aura:

> How extraordinary it was, strange, yes, touching, to see the old lady (they had been neighbors ever so many years) move away from the window, as if she were attached to that sound, that string. . . . She was forced, so Clarissa imagined, by that sound, to move, to go—but where. . . . Why creeds and prayers and mackintoshes? When, thought Clarissa, that's the miracle, that's the mystery; that old lady, she meant, whom she could see going from chest of drawers to dressing-table. (141)

This exquisitely mundane image perfectly reflects the priority Clarissa places on the privacy and independence of every soul. "Somehow one respected that. . . . There was something solemn in it" (140). Yet such separateness does not connote isolation from others, or from life. The old lady's being tied like a string to the pulsing of Big Ben reflects the way all beings and things are bound by the passage of time, and by their own instincts for survival, to keep moving from one room to another. It is the purity and uniqueness of every individual's progress—"here was one room; there another" (141), "[building] it up, first one thing and then another" (160)—which inspires Clarissa's respect and makes her condemn the inadequacy of either love or religion to fathom it, and the hypocrisy of people who insist they do.

It is this shared understanding of the soul's integrity and the cruel egotism of those who infringe upon it which allows for Clarissa's vivid and spontaneous perception of Septimus's suicide. The death itself is linked via numerous images with Clarissa's own experience. Its immediate cause is the intrusion of Dr. Holmes who, says Rezia, "seemed to stand for something horrible" (155) to Septimus, and who Clarissa would label a converter, or one who "forces the soul."

The scene preceding Septimus's suicide is full of reverberating images which connect his consciousness with Clarissa's. As Septimus lies on the sofa in the sitting-room, for instance, he imagines "the sound of water was in the room," and his hand, on the sofa back, was "floating, on the top of the waves, while far away on shore he heard dogs barking and barking far away. Fear no more, says the heart in the body; fear no more" (154). Septimus's perception of floating upon the water is a pointed reverberation of Clarissa's "perpetual sense . . . of being out, out, far out to sea and alone" (11) which, like the echoed line from *Cymbeline*, connotes the same fragile life and preparedness for death.

Clarissa's instinctive understanding of the reasons for Septimus's suicide when she hears of it at her party, and her mental experience of the death itself, build up a remarkable layering of connections. "In the middle of my party, here's death, she thought" (203), voicing her recognition of the centrality of this young man's suicide to the pattern of order she has established with her party. The intensity of her identification with him leads her to experience his death vicariously. "He had thrown himself from a window. Up had flashed the ground; through him, blundering, bruising, went the rusty spikes. There he lay with a thud, thud, thud in his brain, and then a suffocation of blackness" (203). Perceiving instinctively the "obscure evil" of Sir William Bradshaw, having herself once gone to him for advice, Clarissa knows at once how it was. The rape imagery of her vicarious experience of his death (the "area railings" having become "rusty spikes" upon which he is impaled) denotes her recognition of Septimus's suicide as a desperate flight from an "indescribable outrage," a terrible violation of self. Having acted out his death in consciousness ("Indeed she felt it now"), Clarissa understands clearly its cause, and its character as an act of defiance.

Reflecting on her own survival, Clarissa perceives as "her disgrace" the compromise she makes which Septimus does not: "A thing there was that mattered; a thing wreathed about with chatter, defaced, obscured in her own life, let drop every day in corruption, lies, chatter. This he had preserved" (204). It is Clarissa's ability to compromise, though, which enables her to bridge the gap between sanity and insanity, between survival and death. Her parties are her compromise; the tenuous pattern of connections she creates between such disparate individuals as the prime minister, Lady Bruton, Ellie Henderson, Peter Walsh, Sally Seton, even Sir William Bradshaw, are what enable her to endure, however "wreathed about" they are with chatter.

The repeated image of the old lady across the way reflects this idea of survival through affiliation, and, linked as it is with Septimus's death, creates a quadripartite network of connections in which all is brought together. The old man coming down the staircase opposite, who stops and stares at Septimus as he is getting ready to jump from the boarding house window, is an image akin to that of the old lady Clarissa watches, admiring her independence and integrity. Clarissa's "old lady" and Septimus's "old man" can be seen as alter egos for each, as images of the enduring self, one which grows old in accord with the passage of time, but which preserves its integrity, remaining separate and unique but infinitely affiliated with others. This is the possibility for survival Septimus is unable to grasp. Whereas Clarissa feels an affiliation with her neighbor which sustains and supports her, Septimus, trapped in the isolation of madness, is unable to do so. The old man exists only as a neutral, detached observer, whom Septimus recognizes but from whom he is cut off.

In the "little room" Clarissa enters to make sense of her response to Septimus's death, she sees once again the old lady in the room opposite. Suddenly "oh, but how surprising! . . . the old lady stared straight at her" (205). Clarissa makes the connection with the old woman, and the aspect of self she symbolizes, that Septimus could not. As she watches, fascinated, "that old woman, quite quietly, going to bed alone . . . with people still laughing and shouting in the drawing-room" (205), she experiences a sense of connectedness which reaffirms her commitment to life. The young man who had killed himself is transmuted into the old woman putting out her light; thus, "she did not pity him . . . with the clock striking the hour . . . with all this going on" (206). Affiliations with others—with Septimus, with the old lady, with all the individuals at her party, with Richard, Peter, Sally and with herself—are the web which supports her. Very much in line with Gilligan's distinction between masculine and feminine perspectives, Clarissa perceives a "network of connections" which Septimus does not, and this is what allows her to survive.

That supporting "web" is infinitely fragile, however. The blurring of boundaries effected by the Clarissa/Septimus double, above all, makes clear the very fine line between sanity and insanity, life and death. Clarissa's pattern-making, resting as it does on a basis of affiliation between self and others, enables her to live; Septimus's only alienates him further; this is the crucial distinction between them, and it is, of course, partially ascribable to gender. The feminine impulse toward connecting, joining, sustaining relationships (discussed by Gilligan, Chodorow and Miller) is represented as a redemptive force and a "different voice" which needs to be heard. As Elizabeth Abel has pointed out, the elderly nurse of Peter Walsh's "solitary traveller" dream, the woman knitting who seemed "to be the figure of the mother whose sons have been killed in the battles of the world," (65) is an image of this feminine principle, akin to that of Clarissa stitching her dress.[6] The ragged old woman at the subway entrance ceaselessly singing her age-old songs is another such image.

Woolf clearly distinguishes between masculine and feminine dispensations, and she seems to suggest that learning to hear the female voice is a matter of survival. Equally clear is her perception that gender division can be transcended in consciousness. The Clarissa/Septimus double is, above all else, an image of this transcendent consciousness. Through the intermeshing of Septimus's and Clarissa's thoughts and experiences, the divisions between male and female, sanity and insanity, poor and privileged, life and death, appear more and more arbitrary, less and less real. The male/female double of Woolf's novel does more than defy the division of gender; it challenges "life's power to divide."

3

Male/Female Friendship
in *The Needle's Eye*

*"I want her," he said to himself. The words walked into his mind
and stood about there. They shocked him. They were shocking.
He wished instantly, and knew he would continue to wish, that
he had never known. "I want her," himself said again. And then
more fully, more decisively repeated, "I want what she is."*
                                                    The Needle's Eye

Halfway through Margaret Drabble's *The Needle's Eye*, Simon Camish
has this revelation of feeling for Rose Vassiliou (186). The variation in
phrasing from "I want her," with its sexual/romantic connotations, to
the more existentially focused "I want what she is," highlights a significant aspect of this novel's male/female double and its similarity to that
of Woolf's *Mrs. Dalloway*. Like Woolf, Drabble suggests that romantic
attachment is detrimental to male/female bonding, that it raises divisive
barriers (over which are waged sexual/political battles) between men
and women. Drabble, however, appears to suggest that gender barriers
can be transcended and the way cleared for a dynamic and mutually
supportive interaction between male and female within the social environment. In this belief, Drabble is a descendant of Charlotte Brontë,
whose goal in *Jane Eyre* was to construct just such a space, though
within a romantic and marital context.

In *The Needle's Eye* Drabble has created something rather unique in
contemporary fiction: a constructive and long-standing male/female
friendship. That Simon Camish wants what Rose Vassiliou is (and not
the reverse) makes clear the way in which this bond reflects Gilligan's
suggestion as to the benefits of learning to recognize women's different
psychological perspective. What Simon is drawn to in Rose is precisely

those qualities which Gilligan describes as primarily feminine: a capacity for emotional openness, intimacy, and sustained connections with others.

The opening scene of the novel both reveals Simon's estrangement from these qualities and anticipates his attraction to Rose. On his way to a dinner party, Simon stops into an "off-licence" to purchase a bottle of wine for his hostess. As he waits patiently in line, he wonders if his habitual politeness could be called an emotion. "That was how he regarded it, certainly—an emotion that he both feared and understood" (9). Simon is so estranged from his feelings that he has difficulty even identifying them. He describes himself as living in "negation" and as being motivated only by such "emotions" as politeness and obligation.

By contrast, the enthusiasm and pleasure of the elderly woman ahead of him in line makes Simon feel "rejected and excluded and judged" (19). As the woman lingers lovingly over her purchases of Guinness, Players, and fizzy orange, Simon feels "violent waves of nostalgia." He feels he knows this woman's origins: "a world from which he was forever exiled," with its "domestic interiors, its pleasures, its horizons." Enjoying vicariously the woman's involvement, Simon feels "a pang of loss" when she leaves. For him, "there was no point in making any effort" (9–11). This capacity for enjoying the mundane details of experience, which Simon lacks, is precisely what he is drawn to in Rose Vassiliou.

On his first visit to Rose's house, Simon experiences a similar sense of both familiarity and exile. The comfortable clutter and closeness of her home remind Simon of "somewhere intensely remembered," of his grandmother's house, full of objects "well worn, well used, lived with." He is surprised to be pleased at this remembrance since, "after very early infancy," he had found that house "cramped, oppressive . . . and too full of . . . menacing embraces" (43). This first encounter with Rose, in effect, awakens in Simon memories of a previous existence, a previous self, which lived before the characteristic movement (in masculine development) toward separateness and isolation.

With Rose, however, that past emerges stripped of its previous threat. Gazing at Rose in her rocking chair, he notes that "she looked contained within herself . . . not reaching out or pleading in any direction" (43). Though she sought his advice in sorting out the complexities of her divorce and imminent custody dispute, Simon "could sense nothing underground or subversive in her appeal" (44). For these reasons Simon finds himself enjoying something "unusually like contentment" (45) and wishing once again "to find touching, to find chosen, not accidental warmth, to find intimacy and contact" (52).

Rose herself, though, strikes Simon as somehow "untouchable"

(43), one of many suggestions in the novel of the nonsexual nature of their bond and the extent to which its constructiveness is dependent on this. Drabble remarked, in an unusually revealing interview with Nancy Hardin, that she had "desexed" both Rose and Simon slightly and noted, in an interesting personal vein, that she thought this was why Rose was a "better woman than I am" (294). The moral implications of this concept of goodness will be taken up later in this chapter, but it is useful to note here the corrollary between this idea of sexuality as an impediment to goodness and as an obstacle in relationships.

Elsewhere in the Hardin interview, Drabble remarks that "sexual love is completely unreliable. What seems to be a profound matter of the spirit is simply a passing matter of the body" (287). She refers particularly to the failed love between Rose and Christopher, but the same can be said of virtually every marriage in the novel. "I don't know why one gets married" (277), Drabble remarked, a mystery apparently shared by all her characters. Rose's abusive marriage (a history of short-lived passion, beatings and recriminations, and general sexual/political combat); Simon's loveless and empty one; Nick and Diana's marriage of mere social convenience; Rose's neighbor Eileen's brief romantic interlude with a mechanic which leaves her with an unwanted pregnancy, no lover, and no prospects: these comprise the grim backdrop against which Rose and Simon's remarkable bond is represented. Given the overwhelmingly dismal picture of romantic and marital love in the novel, small wonder that their bond, if it is to be a constructive one, is represented as fairly devoid of sexual feeling. Small wonder that, when first alone with Rose, Simon feels it "a vast relief" that he is not called upon to make any sexual advances toward her (43).

The nonsexual nature of their bond is, in fact, stated explicitly by both. Simon, in his infinite, introspective musings upon his attraction to Rose, makes a direct contrast between his perception of her and his sense of the conventionally sexually appealing. Studying Rose and her friend Emily, for instance, Simon remarks upon "how extremely agreeable the two women looked," though neither would be considered beautiful.

> They looked—he found it hard to explain it to himself—they looked complete, they looked like people. So many women, he found, did not look like people at all: they aspired after some image other than the personal. These were the women, though he did not like to think of it, that peopled his fantasies—smooth, shiny, made-up sexy women, wearing underwear under their clothes, provocative, female other . . . There is nothing he would have more disliked than the realisation of his fantasies. (224)

Rose and Emily are somehow exempt from femaleness, the implication being that female equates to something less than, or other than, human. Simon surmises that the reason he finds Rose and Emily so agreeable is precisely because "he did not find them attractive" (225). Of Rose, in fact, Simon remarks that, "It was almost impossible, really, to think of her as a woman, so entirely did she manage to present herself in a neutral light" (164). It is a position Simon both admires and shares, having always presented himself, not strictly as a man, but as "something less dangerous" (164).

Rose also exempts Simon from masculinity. She casually remarks to him that she had "had quite enough of men." Simon observes, without regret or displeasure, "that he was acquitted of the crime of belonging to this rejected category" and adds, significantly, that "perhaps it was the only way to talk to anybody" (164). Even communication requires a certain gender-free perspective.

This idea of sexuality as "dangerous" and as detrimental to bonding is shared by most of the fictions examined here. The implication is that, for genuine male/female bonding to occur, gender constraints must be transcended, and since sexual interaction serves to support and sustain gender division, sexual relation must be avoided. Sexual identity itself, or rather, self-definition based on such identity, must to some extent be transcended as well (as is evident from Rose and Simon's efforts to present themselves in a "neutral" light).

This idea is a corollary to the concept of sexual identity in Woolf's *Mrs. Dalloway*. Clarissa's and Septimus's nonheterosexual bonds with Sally Seton and Evans provided a loosening of gender identity which helped to make possible their psychic connection. Although homosexual experience plays little part in Drabble's novel, with the possible exception of Rose's close friendship with Emily (which, interestingly, Christopher cites as a cause of their divorce), the same principle of nonrestrictive sexual identity as prerequisite to the gender-transcendent bond is evident. One cannot, apparently, think of oneself too determinedly as male or female if one hopes to connect with another across the boundary of gender.

A certain romantic tension is evident between Simon and Rose, however. Simon describes it tentatively, exploratively (as in the opening quote), demonstrating quite obvious confusion. He is very much aware that the words he finds to describe his feelings for Rose ("'I love her,' he said to himself, to try it out, but the words sounded very strange in his head: not untrue, but strange") are inadequate to, even misrepresentative of, their relationship (225). The connotations of "love," in a heterosexual context, are always to some extent erotic. But what other words are there? How else does one describe an intimate bond between a man and a woman except as love?

Drabble, in effect, seems to be contending with the lack of an adequate language, or of an appropriate form, for nonsexual male/female relations. The word "love," as it is ordinarily used to define male/female relationships (like sexual interaction itself), is represented as too limiting, too reductive, as a way of defining the bond between Simon and Rose. Simon, for instance, reflects upon the irony of the fact that he did not find Rose sexually attractive when he had decided he loved her. He is struck by the incongruity of "love" in such a context: "it was a dreadful audacity to think of loving a whole person like that, a whole person so entirely there and so fully existing, a person with a history survived, a person who had made herself so carefully. It was astonishing, it was remarkable" (225). Love, as it is ordinarily conceived between men and women, involves something less than whole persons, apparently. One can only conclude that it is the constraints of gender which detract from this wholeness. Rose and Simon are, in effect, capable of perceiving one another in their entirety because they have to some extent freed themselves of these gender constraints.

Having crossed the division of gender, they had also to traverse the boundary of class difference. They emerged from different social classes: Rose from an affluence built on nineteenth-century styled industrialism, which she renounces (even giving away her inheritance); Simon from a working class environment from which he moves into wealth (due to an ambitious mother and a wealthy marriage). "You're very like me," Rose says to Simon. "But for different reasons," says Simon. "Yes, yes . . . you have risen in the world, and I have sunk. How curious it is" (306). Rose and Simon are both, in a sense, displaced people, situated in a class different from their origins, both having a clear understanding that one can never fully throw off one's roots. "Ridiculous, really," Rose says, "that one can't get rid of what is one's own" (306). Simon calls himself a "masquerader," and reflects that he "had travelled rather too far too quickly." He remarks that "men do not spring out of the earth like soldiers from dragons' teeth, nor do they spring into and out of grammar schools with such abandon" (30–31).

Interestingly, both had chosen marriage partners partially as rejection of their origins: Rose choosing Christopher because he was "one of the dispossessed—doubly so, financially and racially" (87); Simon choosing Julie because of what he perceived as a kind of carefree, wealth-supported innocence and because his mother did not like her. Both learn that one's roots are not so easily cut and that this knowledge carries a burden of responsibility.

Rose and Simon's shared sense of social obligation is, in fact, a significant aspect of their bond. Rose, though retaining enough of her inheritance on which to live modestly, has situated herself firmly on "Middle Road" and is incapable of refusing any claims on her time and energy. Thinking of Rose with the next-door baby on her knee, "stating quite simply that it was not possible to refuse such a service because the baby's grandmother . . . worked for such and such a small sum, on her knees, scrubbing floors, whereas Rose was sitting safely in her chair," Simon understands and concurs with her reasons. Simon's specialization as a barrister in trade union law is a reflection of a similar awareness. "The issue was of such simplicity," he thinks. "Those that have may not reject those that have not" (211).

To Simon, who has conducted his whole life according to "obligation," Rose's discomfort with her wealth and privilege makes perfect sense. One of the things he is drawn to in Rose is her rejection of class comfort and privilege, however futile this rejection may ultimately be. Looking at Rose sipping tea in the Bryanstons' garden, as a paying guest, Simon reflects: "Her stumbling, her pallor, her renunciations, her vinyl sandals—they appeared to him as the human, as the lovely, as the stuff of life itself" (313). This image is in stark contrast with the Bryanston estate's private splendors. It is Rose's very unremarkableness—"an ordinary person" whom "fate had capriciously elected . . . to notoriety" and who "had made the painful journey back to nature by herself, alone—guided by nothing but her own knowledge, against the current" (311) which inspires Simon's respect.

Rose not only puts Simon back in touch with his working class origins, but also, by her example, imbues them with meaning for him. Her capacity for enjoying "cut prices and sunshine and babies in prams" (107) fills Simon with envy ("I wish that I too could arrive at such a state of grace, " he tells her) but, for the first time perhaps, does not exclude him. On the contrary, he takes a vicarious pleasure in such mundane enjoyments as seeing the "chickens and the armchair," a measure of interest and good will which Simon says is "nothing less than a rebirth in [his] nature" (164).

The difference between Rose and Simon's motivations—Simon's emphasis on the forms of things (politeness instead of good will, obligation instead of desire) and Rose's on the spirit—reflects the dichotomy of letter and spirit which is central to the novel's theme. This dichotomy, in fact, comes closest to defining the central contrast between Rose and Simon and the primary function of their bond, which is to mend that gap. On more than one occasion, Rose and Simon discuss this division. At a party, for instance, Simon expounds upon his theory of law: "The law as an institution," Simon says, "is admirable, they've got it all wrong, it's the uses to which it is put that are wrong. It isn't the letter that kills and the spirit that giveth life at all, it's the other way round." What counts, he asserts, is "that there should be a machinery, for doing the things, so that they get done, by those who can, for those who can't." Rose, listening intently, responds personally and with irritation, "You don't believe that, Simon. . . . If it weren't for people like you taking an interest in making the machinery there wouldn't be any. It's ridiculous to pretend that you don't care and that it would all work all right if you didn't. Ridiculous" (257). Rose is, of course, intensely familiar, through her complicated divorce and custody dispute, with the machinery of the law at work, and the extent to which it fails to solve human problems.

Simon and Rose's debate on the spirit and the letter is enacted on several levels, the law itself being only one. Its enactment within a religious context is perhaps most central to the novel's meaning (as its title makes clear). The previous exchange is remarkably similar, for instance, to another conversation they have which marks the first truly personal dialogue between Rose and Simon—and which shows how closely linked in Drabble's novel are the political and the spiritual. Rose is describing to Simon the joy she takes in the mundane details of her life: "I do them all with love. Getting up, drawing the curtains, shopping, going to bed. You know what I mean." Simon responds sharply, "How could I know what you mean . . . when nothing that I do is done with any love at all?" Again, Rose rejects Simon's assertion: "I don't believe you. . . . It's charity, at least, to sit there for so long and listen to me. And charity is a form of love." To Simon's rejoinder that he might have resented every moment, Rose responds that his listening then would have been even kinder. The core of the debate thus emerges: "I thought things didn't count unless one meant them," Simon says. "No, no, not at all," responds Rose, "You've got it wrong. The clashing of the cymbals and the banging of the something or other, you were thinking of, weren't you? And not having charity. But the act counts. See?" (107–8).

Interestingly, Rose seems here to reverse her argument and take up Simon's, affirming the value of letter over spirit, of form over meaning. Yet the reversal, like the division itself, is an artificial one. Rose and Simon's reflection of one another's view leads us to understand that the two really cannot be divided, that one cannot wholly exist without the other. This division, like that of gender, is healed by a negation of its polarity. Simon and Rose's connection across barriers of gender, of class, of relational and spiritual ways of being reveals the essential falseness of such divisions. One is finally only the reflection of the other.

Still, as in *Mrs. Dalloway*, there is a distinction. Like Woolf's novel, *The Needle's Eye* challenges divisions on numerous levels of human existence and suggests—in line again with Gilligan's developmental theory—that more is to be gained from learning to hear the "different voice" of the female than of the male. Rose's representation as inhabiting a "state of grace" and Simon's position primarily as Rose's observer make clear this distinction.

More than any other of Drabble's novels, *The Needle's Eye* is concerned with spiritual themes, particularly with the concept of grace, a term which recurs often in the novel. Drabble appears to be exploring definitions of grace and seeking reasons for its operation in one life and not another. The interaction between Rose and Simon provides the locus of this inquiry.

The definition of grace the novel seems to advance is best described in relation to the Marxist political stance Rose and Simon share. Their comparable rejection of upper-class privilege and their shared sense (in Simon's words) that "there could be no beauty behind a gate marked Private" (313), define this position. Rose's appreciation of "the daily pleasures of streets well trodden, faces well known, small moments of architectural madness and felicity amidst acres of monotony" goes beyond socialism in simple materialist terms, however. "There was some inexplicable grace, in living so" (157), Rose says. Grace involves more than appropriate social placement, obviously, as Simon's joyless background makes clear. It is more Rose's faith in this environment, and her ability to invest it with meaning, which most closely approximates "grace."

Though Simon is able to perceive the state of grace in which Rose lives (whereas everyone else thinks her "mad") and is strongly attracted to it, he is not really able to emulate it. His enjoyment of it remains, at the end of the novel, still largely vicarious. In the Hardin interview, Drabble notes, "Simon is virtuous, although he has never known grace" (285). The reader must wonder if it is to some extent Rose's femaleness which allows for the operation of grace. As in Woolf's novel, there is the suggestion that the feminine capacity for engaging emotionally with others and for weaving a "web of connections" is part of the reason why Rose experiences grace and Simon only virtue.

Not that grace equates with happiness. Drabble, in fact, allows her characters little peace or contentment. The novel's emphasis on social obligation and responsibility to others precludes this. At the end of the novel, Simon virtuously remains in his loveless marriage, anxiously watching Rose for signs of disaffection; and Rose self-sacrificially returns to her marriage, unable to assume the painful burden of separating Christopher from their children. Of Rose's decision to do so, Drabble says she was "choosing between two kinds of grace" and ultimately "choosing the harder way" (284). Her life separated from Christopher is represented as a "selfish grace" which she is impelled (because of her own sense of moral responsibility) to relinquish.

Signifying the extent to which Rose's realities have become Simon's own, of how fully he has entered "into her own land" (216), Simon is in fact instrumental in effecting Rose's reunion with Christopher, in cementing her choice of this harder way. It is he who suggests to Christopher that he "forget about the divorce, and go back and live with her" (280), feeling in so doing that he has been morally right, since it was so "beautifully to his own disadvantage." He took "satisfaction from the thought that any gain would be his own loss" (281–82). Interestingly, Simon's rationale for this self-sacrificial action is very like Rose's for her decision to reunite with Christopher. "She had been right to take him: no ulterior weakness of her own, no sexual craving, had prompted her to do so, she had done it in the dry light of arid generosity, she had done it for others" (378).

Clearly, Simon and Rose are linked in relation to this self-sacrificial instinct, this concept of morality as responsibility to others and as rejection of personal gain, which Gilligan defines as primarily a feminine impulse. Both Rose's and Simon's decisions here can be seen as reflecting Gilligan's suggestion of the potential trap of self-sacrifice which the feminine moral focus on responsibility to others can engender.

Just as their morality is linked, across the boundary of gender, so is their experience of grace. Having been converted to the commonplace grace of Rose's life on Middle Road, Simon's own faith—or his own vicarious experience of grace—is dependent upon its continuance. After Rose's return to her marriage, Simon "watched like a hawk, for signs of cracking, for signs of ruin, for signs of decay. He needed her, he needed her more than ever. He watched her clothes, to see if she would spend money on herself. . . . He watched her face, and the lines of it, to see if she would betray him" (371). What Simon "needs" is precisely what he once said he wanted: he needs "what she is," or rather, he needs her to remain what she is, since his own faith has been propagated upon hers.

Rose also needs what Simon is. Though she never speaks to Simon about Christopher or her marriage after her return, "she desired his approbation, passionately. It was her strongest emotional need, and one that by its very nature she could take no move to satisfy" (376). Clearly, some portion of Rose's faith is propagated upon Simon, upon his acceptance and understanding of her choices. Having been unique in his recognition of the spiritual calm and commonplace richness of her self-determined life, Simon's continued acceptance is uniquely important to her.

The interconnectedness of Rose and Simon's lives, as represented in this mutual need for each to be who and what they are, is perhaps the strongest indication of the extent to which Rose and Simon comprise a male/female double. Meeting across boundaries of gender, class, and psychological perspective, they appear to carve out and to inhabit a unique social space within a larger social framework of destructive sexual politics, of interclass antagonism, and of spiritual bereftness.

Though situated within a very different context from Woolf's *Mrs. Dalloway*, Drabble's novel shares a similar confrontive approach to the divisions which separate human beings and effects a similar, if partial, success. Like Woolf's text also, *The Needle's Eye* carries the suggestion that feminine interactive capacities, fostered by distinctly gender-defined psychological development, provide women with more effective patterns for the ordering of their social and personal (and, in *Needle's Eye*, spiritual) lives. In *Mrs. Dalloway*, this suggestion is more forceful, implying a gender-defined difference in sheer survival ability. In Drabble's novel too, however, the image of Rose Vassiliou's grace-imbued life carries a similar message about the importance of hearing the female voice.

4

The Male Muse in *The Diviners*

Also, thou shalt not oppress a stranger; for ye know the heart of a
stranger, seeing ye were strangers in the land of Egypt.

Exodus 23:9

Margaret Laurence notes, in her Foreword to *Heart of a Stranger*, that this
verse from Exodus has always been meaningful to her, on a number of
levels. Having lived in England, Ghana, and Somaliland, as well as in
her native Canada, having traveled widely, Laurence knows what it is
to be the outsider. She has learned that oldest and most important
lesson of the traveler: that the experience of other countries and other
peoples teaches one more about oneself than about anything else. That
she returned to Canada in her fiction ten years before she in fact went
home to stay reflects the way in which the experience of the stranger
and the perspective afforded by distance are central to Laurence's writing. She sees that outsider's view as in the very nature of writing: for in
the writer's attempt to gain entrance to the minds of characters, "part
of the heart remains that of a stranger," a "perpetual traveller," in
"those strange lands of the heart and spirit" (vii–viii). That one learns
about the self from the other, acquires an appreciation of one's own
country from visiting others, becomes reconciled to and transcends
one's past seemingly by leaving it behind: these are dichotomies central
to Laurence's fiction.

This metaphor of the "stranger," which is so central to Laurence's
understanding of herself and her craft, also reverberates on the level of
gender. For it is a frequent motif in Laurence's fiction that her central
female characters define themselves, in very significant ways, by reference to the "otherness" of the male. Self-definition hinges upon definition of the other, thus blurring the boundary between self and other,
and because this definition traverses gender, between female and male.

The frequent male/female doubles in Laurence's novels reflect this emphasis upon transcending the gender-bound self in order better to define self. For Laurence's female characters, traversing the boundary of gender plays an important part in establishing identity.

The developmental story of Morag Gunn in *The Diviners* appears even to suggest that identification with maleness is a creative necessity. Although Morag identifies herself as female (learning much, for example, from the experiences of Eva Winkler and Fan Brady), in building and sustaining her creative energy, in learning to "divine" from her past a vital and enduring self, male models appear to play a much more significant role. Morag's interaction with Jules Tonnerre, the male "double" figure of this novel, assists in crucial ways her development as female artist. Functioning as creative guide, or nurturer, the male figure in this novel could be described as a male muse (or "shaman" in the lexicon of *The Diviners*). Very much in keeping with Laurence's concept of the "stranger," the female protagonist of *The Diviners* is assisted in defining and expressing her creative self through identification with the male.

On the surface, at least, this conception of gender is similar to Woolf's aesthetic image of the "androgynous mind"; *The Diviners*, in fact, could be viewed as a fictionalized treatment of its development in the female writer. Laurence's perspective, however, is more optimistic. Her novel suggests not only that the restrictiveness of gender constraints can be transcended on the level of social interaction, but also that it can be a source of creative support for the female artist.

The Diviners could be interpreted as illustrating Gilligan's assertions as to the mutual gain of recognizing male/female developmental difference from the other side: showing not what male may learn from female (as does Drabble's *The Needle's Eye*), but what female may learn from male. In accord with Gilligan's suggestions, much of what Morag Gunn learns from Jules Tonnerre has to do with independence, self-assertion, and individual creative expression. For Morag, as well as for other of Laurence's female characters, transcending the separateness of gender, and integrating aspects of the "other" into the self, is often represented—and this is an interesting contrast with Woolf's fiction—as a matter of survival.

Survival is, in fact, a central theme of *The Diviners*. Like her compatriot, Margaret Atwood, Laurence sees the writer's personal quest for self-definition and the national quest for autonomous identity as parallel: to resist domination by other powers, to reject the position of victim, and to claim one's own distinctive identity and heritage. Significantly, Laurence adds, the task is also "to recognise our legends" and "to give shape to our myths" (*Heart of a Stranger,* 242). For Laurence's characters, surviving nearly always entails a coming to terms with the past and an uncovering of personal and communal history. The "river that flows both ways," an image central to *The Diviners,* symbolizes this sense of past and present as indivisible, and of life not as a linear progression from then to now but as a fluid, dynamic interrelation between former and current experience, past and present selves. Defining the present self is contingent upon knowing the self of the past or, to use another central metaphor, upon "divining" from the past a source of creative energy.

Transcendence of gender constraints plays a central role in facilitating this identification of the self as residing in an experiential continuum between past and present. Frequently in Laurence's fiction the perspective afforded by the "other" gender assists female characters in acknowledging some buried or denied aspect of themselves. In earlier Laurence novels, *The Stone Angel* and *The Fire Dwellers,* such interactions are evident. They are, in effect, doubles akin to Jules and Morag in *The Diviners,* though not as fully developed; and they reflect Laurence's long-standing interest in this type of cross-gender interaction.

In a brief but crucial scene in *Stone Angel,* Hagar Shipley has an encounter with a kind of second self in the middle-aged insurance salesman, Murray F. Lees, from which she emerges better able to cope with the imminence of her death. The interaction takes place in a very dark seaside shack where Hagar, having left her son's house because of his plans to institutionalize her, has sought shelter. In the darkness, unable to see one another clearly or, indeed, to perceive any boundaries or divisions, they share their personal histories—histories which are remarkably similar. Murray's tale of grief and loss (a dead son, an embittered marriage) parallels Hagar's own unresolved grief, guilt and anger. Thinking over to herself the tragic accident that claimed her own son, she is surprised by Murray's sympathetic response to find she has spoken it aloud. Speaking to Murray is, for Hagar, only another form of speaking to herself. In a confused, early morning moment, Hagar mistakes Murray for her lost son, and he, giving her the gift of a lie, accords her the forgiveness she needs; in relieving her burden of guilt, his own is somewhat eased. His grief awakens hers; his equal loss allows her to transcend the embittered egotism of her own, and finally to expiate it. Thus Hagar recognizes "it was a kind of mercy I encountered him" (253). Leaving with her son, whom Murray had called, Hagar is finally able to prepare for death: "Odd," she thinks, "only now do I see that what's going to happen can't be delayed indefinitely" (254).

There is a similar interaction in *The Fire Dwellers.* As in *Stone Angel,* the double here functions to assist the central female character over a difficult crisis period in her life. Stacey Cameron, salesman's wife and mother of four, is approaching forty and feeling alienated from herself. She enters into a brief affair with a much younger man named Luke, whom she meets on the beach after having, like Hagar, "run away from home." Their conversation, too, is more like shared internal monologue, and the authenticity of the male figure is also decidedly undercut. "You're real? You're not real. I'm imagining," Stacey muses; he responds, "You're not imagining. But maybe I'm not that real, so don't count on it" (187). Luke represents an alternative self, the independent, unrestricted one Stacey feels divided from and fears having lost. He offers her an opportunity to reclaim it, not only physically (by joining him on a journey to the north), but also psychologically, by acknowledging, and literally embracing, that other self she has been divided from by too many years of "kinder, kinde and kirsche."

As for Jules and Morag in *The Diviners*, the sexual interaction here is intended to represent a psychological union as well—not so much between man and woman as between masculine and feminine aspects of the one female self. Luke remains largely a shadow figure, an alternative self, the one Stacey might have been had she not built up the network of family and community connections she now recognizes she does not choose to sever. "If I had two lives, I would [accompany him north]" (236), Stacey says, implying that she, in a sense, almost does. Luke returns to her a "suggestion of choice," something with which, in her middle-class housewife situation, she had lost touch. Though Luke goes north, and Stacey returns with a greater sense of commitment to her family, she often has the feeling that "Luke is walking beside her, saying 'it's okay, baby . . . I'm with you there'" (253).

In both these fictions, the male double serves as an alternative self which fosters self-knowledge and life-acceptance for the central female character. Its function is much the same in *The Diviners*, though it is developed further here. Jules Tonnerre has none of the "shadow" quality of Murray or Luke; he is a fully developed character with a personality and a personal history which, though certainly paralleling those of the female character, are also distinct from them. Not surprisingly, in *The Diviners*, where the double is most central and the cross-gender connection most profound, the female hero is also most clearly defined.

The Diviners is at bottom the developmental story of a female writer; the writing of fiction is both its subject and its method. In this way it is strikingly similar to the fiction of Doris Lessing, particularly *The Golden Notebook*. Like the female hero of Lessing's novel, Morag Gunn grows into self-awareness and creative self-expression as a writer through the creation of fictions. So it is with the development of the male/female double in Laurence's novel: it centers on the discovering, the constructing, and the sharing of fictions.

As the novel itself revolves around the telling of stories, and, in fact, ends with the devising of its title (like the circular first line which concludes *The Golden Notebook*), so the relationship between Morag and Jules revolves around the sharing of their stories. The stories are primarily not of their personal but of their historical past, emerging from their very different cultural backgrounds: Morag's of her Highland Scots heritage; Jules of his part Indian/part French, or Metis, ancestry. They receive these stories, altered and elaborated upon by many retellings, from their fathers, both of whom are, in their ways, "scavengers" and "diviners."

Morag's father, Christie, is the town garbage collector, dragging away to the "nuisance grounds" all the refuse of others' lives with which, like a misbegotten prophet, he has the gift of foretelling: "from their garbage shall ye know them," he tells Morag. Jules's father, Lazarus, denied a livelihood by town prejudice against "halfbreeds," as poor as his biblical namesake, scrounged and scratched out a means of survival, despite total ostracism from the Manawaka community. Only his native skills of hunting and trapping enabled him to survive and to feed his many children. For Lazarus, as for Christie (and for the son and daughter they reared), stories of past familial and racial glories nurture a self both creative and resilient. Though victimized by circumstances, the self these fictions support defies victimization, almost literally allowing them to endure.

It is the receiving of these stories from their fathers, and the importance to each of a sense of self extending into and emerging from the past, which forms the basis of the bond between Morag and Jules. The knife and plaid-pin "talismans" given to them by their fathers, oddly exchanged by circumstance, signify this shared sense of historical selfhood and the extent to which those selves interrelate.

Many of Morag's and Jules's stories are, in fact, alternative versions of the same history. "Christie's Tale of Piper Gunn and the Rebels," passed down to Morag, and "Skinner's Tale of Lazarus's Tale of Rider Tonnerre" discuss the same events from different sides, though with at times widely divergent details. And both differ from the accepted historical accounts. "History" is shown to be, in effect, only another fiction, wholly relative, its function to be primarily the stuff of myth, which mythmakers Morag and Jules use in the construction of their past and present selves. "Morag's Story of Christie's Story" tells how the heroic Piper Gunn rallied the Sutherlanders with the music of his bagpipes to oust the upstart halfbreeds from the fort along the Red River. Unlike the history books which credited the English with this expulsion (and all successive ones) and presented the Scots as only a part of their forces, the story Morag is told attributes the victory entirely to Scots valor and initiative. Jules, with his Metis background, tells a different story, about how Rider Tonnerre, with his magical horse Roi du Lac and his trusty rifle La Petite, led the Metis in a valiant fight to protect their lands and their hunting rights. The Metis leader, Riel, is described, alternatively, as a short, crazy halfbreed who incited his people to insurrection and was eventually hanged, or, in Jules's/Lazarus's version, as a divinely inspired leader, the "Prophet," a full seven feet tall, who fought against tremendous odds to save his people's way of life.

Both Jules and Morag are storytellers—Jules in song, Morag in prose—and for both the telling of stories is a way of defining self. The fictions they relate are parallel ones, running along the same historical path, yet divergent, representing alternative and clearly supplementary accounts. In a novel wherein much of what one is is bound up with where one comes from, it is clear that the selves revealed by these fictions are as parallel and cooperative as the fictions themselves. Jules and Morag are separate selves with distinct personal histories, but each represents for the other an aspect of self which must be acknowledged.

Morag, though, resists the bond with Jules, not so much because his history conflicts with hers (indeed, they fill each other's out), but because he represents the self she is trying to escape, the self rooted in a small prairie town. The quest for identity in her Scots ancestry is largely an evasion of this self. Throughout her adolescence and early adulthood, Morag considers it a matter of survival to deny her personal origins, her most immediate history, having not yet learned (as Laurence says in an article on her own hometown of Neepawa) that "my long ago families came from Scotland and Ireland, but . . . my true roots were here" (*Heart of a Stranger*, 244); that "I would carry the land and town all my life within my skull, that they would form the mainspring and source of the writing I was to do, wherever and however far away I might live" (241–42). Jules is, above all else, a reminder of that Manawaka self Morag seeks to deny. He is the taproot to the creative source she has not yet recognized. Thus it is after going to college, when memories of Jules threaten to surface, that Morag reiterates her resistance like a chant: she "will not will not think of it . . . refuses to think of it" (187).

In her most self-destructive act of denial, she marries the English Brooke Skelton, "aristocratic" college professor who finds attractive her "mysterious, nonexistent past" (195), and who, in fact, requires a denial of that past. She willingly acquiesces: "Could she be exactly what he wants? What does he want? She will find out. She will conceal everything about herself which he might not like" (196). She constructs in this marriage a fiction of virtually a whole new self, complete with cultured vocabulary, beauty-salon hairstyle, and sherry-sipping refinements. With Brooke, she asserts, she is happy, "and anything else—Manawaka and that—it's over. It doesn't exist" (198).

This denial of past requires a denial of her bond with Jules; Jules is, in effect, that past. Morag allows Brooke's assumption of her virginity to pass uncorrected though she had, in fact, experienced her sexual initiation with Jules. Morag knows that "if she tells him about Jules, he will leave her" (199). Any acknowledgment of Jules would disrupt the fiction of her carefully constructed present self, like a pulled thread unraveling an entire fabric. When the fiction does indeed unravel, Morag's sense of self refusing to remain static and buried, it is appropriately Jules who again provides the rite of passage.

Equally appropriate is the theme of her first novel which she completes at the same time her marriage is disintegrating. *Spear of Innocence* is largely about the destructiveness of naiveté, the false benignity of innocence. Coming painfully to herself, Morag begins to recognize the deception of her married life and its cost: that it was a self-denying fiction instead of a self-defining one. The writing of this fiction was transformative; as it was through fictions (of Piper Gunn, of Rider Tonnerre) that Morag first defined herself, so is that self reclaimed.

Contact with her Manawaka self, her true roots, is central to that reclamation, and Jules provides the taproot connection which helps make it possible. Running into him by accident on a Toronto street, not having seen him in ten years, Morag takes Jules home with her for dinner. She feels a strong need for physical contact with him: "she is not making a play. She wants only to touch him, someone from a long long way back, someone related to her in ways she cannot define and feels no need of defining" (267).

The sexual interaction which follows suggests more an establishing of contact with her alienated self than with Jules himself. The blurring of boundaries between self and other which is characteristic of the male/female double is most complete here. Jules, in effect, represents the self from which she is divided and is the vehicle for its reclamation. "This joining is being done," Morag thinks, as "some debt or answer to the past, some severing of inner chains which have kept her bound and separated from part of herself" (271). Jules says to Morag afterward, in recognition of what she is doing and his role within it, "Magic. You were doing magic, to get away. . . . I'm the shaman, eh?" (273). In his role as conductor through a rite of passage (from the self of false fiction to that of "true" fiction), Jules serves as a kind of shaman, or healer, for Morag—not through the imposition of his power, but as a focus for Morag's own. As second self, as double, Jules fosters that connection with self which will empower Morag to take up her new life.

Morag's choice to become pregnant by Jules, or rather to "not do anything to try not to" (279), reflects this newly generated self which union with Jules precipitates. Strikingly similar to Margaret Atwood's *Surfacing*, pregnancy here represents a break from past deceptions, past victimization, and the emergence of an entirely new self. The daughter Morag bears, named Pique after Jules's sister Piquette who died in a fire at the Tonnerre shack, is a tangible symbol of Morag's acknowledgment of, and union with, the self she had been fleeing.

It bears mentioning that unlike most male/female doubles in women's fictions, the bond between Jules and Morag involves sexual interaction. Why this is included in Laurence's fiction, when the fictions of other women writers appear to suggest that sexual relationship disrupts the double bond, is a significant question. Certainly part of the answer lies in the peculiar psychological character of sexual interactions between Jules and Morag, such as the one just described. Most often physical interaction is intended to represent—as it did in the previous instance—more a creative, even healing, psychological union, acted out for the most part within the psyche of the female character, than strictly a sexual union between man and woman. Sexual interaction appears to be, in effect, a metaphor for the unification of the female artist-self, which is the primary focus of the novel.

This is all very well, one might object, but why then, if Jules and Morag's interaction is so creative, do they only meet every ten years or so? Clearly, Laurence's fiction, too (like Drabble and Woolf), suggests that there are limits on the extent to which erotic relation remains constructive. Though Morag and Jules express a strong sexual attraction, the erotic aspect of their relationship is actually undercut. Pressed by Pique to define her feelings for Jules ("Did you love him?"), Morag finds adequate words elusive: "I guess you could say love. I find words more difficult to define than I used to. I guess I felt—feel—that he was related to me in some way" (235). The word "love," with its romantic/erotic connotations, misses the mark as definition of Jules and Morag's bond. It is apparently too risky for them even to see each other with any regularity. Otherwise "it'll turn out bad" (179), Jules says. They share an unspoken understanding that anything more than infrequent visits would disrupt their bond.

The kind of connection revealed by Jules's and Morag's shared fictions is more to the point. After the birth of Pique, the sharing of those stories takes on another dimension, with a stronger emphasis on Jules's fictions and his manner of telling them, in song. Jules had intended to share his songs with Morag when she spent three weeks with him after leaving her husband, but decided the time wasn't right: "I don't guess you'd hear them, really" (279), he tells Morag. The emphasis being on Morag's reclamation of self, the time was wrong for the expression of Jules's individuality.

Their next meeting, though, when Pique is five and Jules visits her and Morag in Vancouver for two months (their longest time together), shows Pique being initiated into Tonnerre history with "The Ballad of Jules Tonnerre," Jules's song for his grandfather who fought with Riel, and into Jules' different way of creating fictions, which eventually becomes her own. Pique is excited by Jules's songs: "I want a song for me, Dad. Hey, would you?" Jules responds, "Maybe someday . . . or maybe you'll make up a song for me" (346). Pique, bearer of both their names, offspring of their connection, must share both their histories, express both ways of being. Raised on stories—Morag's telling of Christie's stories and her own; Jules's telling of Lazarus's stories and his own—Pique comes to share their common means of defining and sustaining the self: through fictions of the past, of familial and communal histories, and of past selves.

Jules expresses a brutal insistence, when he sees Pique at fifteen, that she have the facts of his family tragedies, unmediated and unsoftened. He tells her not only the old stories of Lazarus and Piquette, but also the ones of more recent tragedies: of his brother Paul's death by drowning as a canoe guide up north; of his sister Val's death, from booze and speed, on the streets of Vancouver. "Why did you have to tell me? Why did you have to?" Pique cries, not wanting to own these stories as a part of her past. Jules's response makes clear the major purpose of narrative for him: that it may prevent the repetition of history. "Too many have died. . . . Too many, before it was time. I don't aim to be one of them. And I don't aim for you to be neither" (430). If knowing one's history enhances self-definition, it may also offer self-protection.

Thus fictions operate as a kind of talisman, protecting one from harm, helping one to know oneself. In this last meeting of the three together, with Pique on the verge of adulthood, and Morag and Jules in middle age, all talismans are exchanged, all their shared history unfolded. The knife and plaid-pin, symbols of Jules's and Morag's alternative histories, are returned to rightful owners. Each has held this charm, this last gift from their fathers, in safekeeping for the other, not knowing its meaning or origin, but carrying it out of some kind of faith in its significance.

All mysteries are now revealed: the obscure marking on the hilt of the knife Morag was given by Christie is the letter T for Tonnerre; the foreign-looking scribble on the silver plaid-pin Jules was given by Lazarus is the Gaelic motto, "My hope is constant in thee." The exchanged talismans are symbolic of Jules's and Morag's interrelation, the way in which their selves, like their histories, both reflect and supplement one another. This final exchange, then, suggests that the identity of each has taken its final shape and that the double-bond has completed its central task. A tangible symbol of the other is no longer needed, for the other has become part of the self. Each has owned and profited from the fictions of the other.

Pique, of course, adds a new layer to that canon of fictions. Like her mother and father before her, she makes pilgrimages, seeks her roots. At eighteen, she hitchhikes to Manawaka and to the Tonnerre homestead at Galloping Mountain; the new sense of identity she acquires from this journey is reflected in "Pique's Song" which tells of "the valley and mountain that hold my name." Carrying on her parents' tradition of sharing fictions, Pique sings her song for Morag, who later passes it on to Jules. She takes on, too, her parents' painful sense of lost languages: Jules of French and Cree, Morag of Gaelic. From a book, she learns Louis Riel's last song, written in prison before he was hanged, and she has a friend teach her the French words. Ignorant of their meaning, still she learns them and passes them along (like the talismans of Jules and Morag), perceiving as her parents did the necessity of retaining this link with the past.

The interplay of all these fictions—Old Jules's, Riel's, Christie's, Lazarus's, Morag's, Jules's and finally Pique's—forms the stuff of which selfhood is understood and defined: not in isolation, but in connection; not only in the present, but also in the past. All perform the magic of "divining": locating a creative source which nurtures the self among the relics and refuse of the past. It is this central metaphor, finally, which explains, not only the bond between Jules and Morag, but also the interconnection of fictions throughout the novel.

In the "present" of the novel, Morag has a neighbor named Royland, ex-Bible puncher and rambler, current diviner of wells, whom she also perceives as a kind of shaman. Fascinated by his divining, seeking some knowledge from him she cannot even define, Morag accompanies him every time he is called upon to locate a wellspring. It is the secret of divining she is after, some explanation of this apparently inherent talent. Royland is, in fact, the culminating image of the male muse figure which has played a consistently integral part in Morag's development. He is another version of Christie, with his "telling of the garbage," and of Jules who through a kind of magic helps her to leave her false marriage and reclaim her self.

Though not causally related, there is an interesting parallel between Jules's death and Royland's loss of divining power, which occurs immediately afterward. The proximity of these events, and the fact that both are called "shaman," supports the complementarity of their roles in relation to Morag. In fact, Morag's understanding during her last visit to Jules, when he is dying of throat cancer—for a singer/storyteller, a comparable loss of divining power—is similar to the secret she finally learns from Royland. Though Jules is dying, Morag sees there is "no way of talking to him differently . . . no way of saying everything she would like." For the first time, though, she realizes that "maybe none of it really needed saying, after all" (444); it is a perception unlike Morag's usual verbal, analytical self and very like Jules, who communicated little verbally and for whom "all the things he could never bring himself to say . . . found their way into song" (346).

What Morag learns from Royland's loss of power reflects a similar kind of acceptance of the inexplicable. Royland explains that, though he never understood the divining, it requires no special talent and, in fact, one can learn to do it: "You don't have to have the mark of God between your eyebrows. Or if you do, quite a few people have it." All that is needed is a persistence, a certain faith in its working, and an ability to "get over wanting to explain it" (452). Morag recognizes that "she had known it all along, but not really known."

This knowledge affords Morag a new ease with and acceptance of her own style of divining, on the page. Though she would never know whether her "magic tricks" actually worked or not (unlike Royland with his visible wells), "in a sense, it did not matter. The necessary doing of the thing—that mattered" (452). Morag's need to define her creative source has disappeared, along with the need for a shaman to put her in touch with it. Relying finally more confidently on her own ability to "divine," she has, in effect, become her own shaman. The male muse has been internalized as her own creative energy; the other has become the self.

5

Return to the Myth in Fictions by Le Guin, Bryant, and Tiptree

*But it was from the difference between us, not from the affinities
and likenesses, but from the difference, that that love came: and
it was itself the bridge, the only bridge, across what divided us.*
                                        The Left Hand of Darkness

A number of contemporary female writers of science fiction and fantasy
have demonstrated a keen awareness of the constraints of gender and
have explored ways of transcending them. What such fictions make
clear is that the fantasy genre provides abundant space for challenging
a wide range of cultural divisions to a much fuller extent than is possible
in mimetic fiction. Women writers' fuller participation in the scifi/fan-
tasy genre in recent years, and their unique use of it to challenge gender
constraints, suggests a movement back into the mythic realm of Emily
Brontë's *Wuthering Heights*. Their frequent representation of male/fe-
male bonds, often existing quite literally outside patriarchy, is strongly
reminiscent of the mythic, extrasocial space in which Catherine and
Heathcliff were situated.

I focus in this chapter on three texts, by Le Guin, Bryant, and
Tiptree, as representative of female writers' explorations in this genre.
Interestingly, all three of the novels—again like Brontë's fiction—have
male narrators, a similarity which, though apparently coincidental in
terms of selection, raises some provocative questions about authorial
method and intent. Does the male narrator function, as it does to some
extent in Brontë's novel, as a veil concealing the challenge to patriarchy
that the fictions represent? Since strictures on female writing, though
lessened, are still culturally evident, it is certainly possible that in these
contemporary novels the use of a male narrator may in a similar way

disguise the author's antipatriarchal intent and, to some extent, allow her to express it more freely behind a masculine disguise. One of the science fiction writers I discuss, James Tiptree Jr., like the Brontës, utilized the "disguise" of a masculine pseudonym.

I believe the male narrator suggests other motives, though, which are similar to those of some of the "realistic" fictions I have discussed. In all three of the novels, the male character-narrator's experience of alien culture and consciousness, and his transformative growth as a result of this experience, best defines the central action of the narrative. Utilizing a male narrator and protagonist thus may suggest—as it does in Drabble's *The Needle's Eye* and, in a different way, in Woolf's *Mrs. Dalloway*—that masculine modes of perception limit and divide more stringently than feminine, and that learning to hear the feminine voice (since the growth of these male protagonists is fostered by bonding with one of "alien" gender) is central to cultural change. Women fantasy writers' use of male narrator-protagonists thus may suggest two things: a sense that masculine perception must be radically transformed in order for cultural divisions to be healed, and an optimistic belief that it can be changed, given enough space and sufficient cultural sanction.

In the essay "Is Gender Necessary?," Ursula K. Le Guin called her creation of the ambisexual Gethenians in *The Left Hand of Darkness* (1969) a "thought-experiment" designed, on one level at least, to determine what truly differentiates men and women. "I eliminated gender," she explains, "to find out what was left. Whatever was left would be, presumably, simply human. It would define the area that is shared by men and women alike" (153). Her question is, in effect: what happens to our conception of humanness, and of human interaction, when gender is eliminated?

The result of this experiment is not a utopian society; it is, however, a world free from war, slavery, or other of the blatant forms of oppression with which we are familiar. Le Guin clearly sees rigid gender divisions as directly related to our largest social problems. If we were "socially ambisexual," Le Guin asserts, our central problem would not be what it is now: "the problem of exploitation . . . of the woman, of the weak, of the earth. Our curse is alienation, the separation of yang from yin. Instead of a search for balance and integration, there is a struggle for dominance. Divisions are insisted upon, interdependence is denied" (159). Le Guin's insistence on balance and interdependence instead of hierarchy and opposition reflects again the characteristically feminine moral stance Gilligan describes. As unifying symbol of this moral perspective, the yin/yang image recurs throughout Le Guin's novel, and defines its title.

As is true for most feminists (whether or not so acknowledged), the personal-political division is another ideological dualism Le Guin denies. Thus she portrays her moral vision of interdependence and connection in the microcosm of a single human relationship, which is, according to the terms of my definition, a double. Le Guin has, in fact, insisted that her original conception of this novel had nothing to do with plot or theme, let alone moral view. A book comes to her "as a person," she says, and in the case of *Left Hand of Darkness* it came to her in the image of two persons, "small figures, remote, in a tremendous waste landscape of ice and snow." They were "pulling a sledge or something over the ice, hauling together" (100). It is the image of these two figures, sex unspecified, which is the seed of her novel, both its starting place and its goal.

When asked what she saw as the central, ongoing theme of her work, Le Guin answered, spontaneously, "marriage," and she went on to remark that she had not yet written a novel worthy of that tremendous theme (133). Minus its institutionalized characteristics, marriage is an appropriate metaphor for the type of self-to-self connection, or, in other words, the double, which is the center of this novel, and the healing of divisions this double reflects.

To an extent, Le Guin achieves her image of "marriage," her vision of yin/yang balance, within a single person in the novel, the ambisexual Gethenian, Therem Harth rem ir Estraven. When Genly Ai describes the yin/yang symbol to Estraven, explaining its balance of light and dark, good and evil, male and female, he exclaims, "It is yourself, Therem. Both and one. A shadow on snow" (267).

This image of harmonious balance, though, is qualified by the fact that Estraven generally emerges as more masculine than feminine. Le Guin herself saw this as "a real flaw in the book," acknowledging that "for the reader, I left out too much. One does not see Estraven as a mother, with his children, in any role which we automatically perceive as 'female': and therefore, we tend to see him as a man"—instead of the way she saw him, "as man and woman, familiar and different, alien and utterly human" (*Language*, 158). How much responsibility for this "flaw" rests with Le Guin's narration and how much with her readers' perception—because we are "culturally conditioned to perceive as male" the roles Estraven was cast into—is difficult to determine. Certainly, though, Estraven is intended to represent a model for the transcendence of restrictive divisions in perception which are imposed by gender. Before Genly Ai and Estraven can achieve their double-bond, Genly Ai must confront the challenges posed by this model. Within the framework of this novel, Le Guin seems to suggest that true "marriage" (in the larger sense she intends) is only possible when gender constraints are transcended.

Consistent, then, with Le Guin's original conception of *Left Hand* (the two sexless figures hauling a sledge) the major theme of this novel is the development of an intensely interactive relationship between Genly and Estraven. To purify this focus, Le Guin separates her two major characters from all familial, social, national, and even geographical ties. She places them alone together, utterly isolated and absolutely interdependent, on the elevated arctic plateau of Gethen, the Gobrin Ice. This long section is the real heart of the novel, for which all preceding narrative events serve as preface. A more blatant example of apatriarchal space, the terrain which Pratt suggests is necessary for unconventional relationships, could hardly be imagined.

Le Guin takes pains to emphasize the completeness of her characters' exile. Estraven notes in his journal that "up here on the Ice each of us is singular, isolate, I as cut off from those like me, from my society and its rules, as he from his. . . . We are equals at last, equal, alien, alone" (232). Significantly, both are exiled because of their belief in connections with others which transcend cultural boundaries. Estraven is the first of his world to understand Genly's message of interplanetary cultural exchange, symbolized by the Ekumen, and thus is accused of treason for offending Gethenian nationalism. Their sharing of this belief in cooperation above competition, in network above hierarchy, prepares them to occupy that apatriarchal space together and to venture upon the more personal transcendence of boundary signified by gender.

This final transcendence is primarily Genly's task as it is he, the single-sexed, masculine Terran, who is most constrained by gender roles, and thus most confused by their denial. A significant portion of the novel shows Genly struggling with his gender-based expectations of others and definitions of self. He continually attempts to categorize the Gethenians (who are always both male and female) according to gender, in order to know how to interact with them, and is continually frustrated in his efforts. It is only through enforced exile with Estraven that he gradually becomes aware of these limitations in his thinking and the degree to which he is cut off from others—as well as from himself—because of them. At one point on the Ice, Genly tries to explain to Estraven about gender, and in so doing confronts his own confusion. He tells Estraven that "the heaviest single factor in one's life is whether one's born male or female," that, in most places, "it determines one's expectations, activities, outlook, ethics, manners—almost everything" (234).

The confusing results of such division begin to dawn on Genly when he attempts to answer Estraven's question about how women are different from men. After much fumbling, and several confused observations such as "women tend to eat less," he concludes, "Harth, I can't tell you what women are like. . . . Women are more alien to me than you are. With you I share one sex, anyhow" (235). But, of course, he doesn't. This inability to see Estraven as he is, both man and woman, and neither, is the result of Genly's gender-constrained perception; and it is this which must be transcended for real connection between self and other to be possible.

The transcendence finally occurs in "On the Ice" and is appropriately presented in an image of birth. This chapter represents the very core of Le Guin's novel, the epiphany of bonding between selves which she identifies as her ongoing subject. At chapter beginning, Genly Ai, in his retrospective narration, tells how sometimes, when falling asleep "in a dark, quiet room," he experiences for a moment "a great and treasurable illusion of the past." At such moments, he says, he knows without doubt "what the real center of [his] life is, that time which is past and lost and yet is permanent." That time-transcendent moment in Genly's past is located in the tent he shared with Estraven on their journey across the Ice.

He recalls the sensual details of that intimately shared space amid the darkness and desolation: the invisible wall of a tent that leans up over his face; the stove which exists only as "a sphere of heat, a heart of warmth"; the "dampness and confining cling" of his sleeping bag; and the barely audible sounds of blowing snow and Estraven's breathing in sleep. Genly says of himself and Estraven: "we are inside, the two of us, in shelter, at rest, at the center of all things. Outside, as always, lies the great darkness, the cold, death's solitude" (240). The heavy, sensual, womb-like imagery of this shared experience, which Genly can only describe later as "joy," is striking in its intensity. It is as if Estraven and Genly occupy this womb-space together, utterly isolated from others yet intimately connected to each other and to life.

They are womb-brothers, or rather, in Le Guin's gender framework here, womb-brothers/sisters. Compelled by the intimacy of their shared exile, challenged by the close and constant example of Estraven's ambisexuality, Genly is finally able to transcend his divisive gender constructs and to recognize his friend as brother/sister, as fellow being, and even as lover. He emerges from this "womb" able to establish a relationship with Estraven on a new and deeper plane of connection. He is able to see Estraven in a way "[he] had always been afraid to see, and had pretended not to see," as a "man who was a woman, a woman who was a man." The fear was gone, and what he was left with at last was "acceptance of him as he was." This acceptance, and the intimate connection it made possible, Genly says, "might as well be called, now as later, love" (248).

Sexual tension is a part of this love, although, as in Laurence's fiction, it is carefully controlled. While Genly and Estraven are alone on the Ice, Estraven goes through "kemmer," that recurrent period in Gethenian sexuality during which the usually dormant sexual impulse becomes active. It is partly the sexual tension emerging from this, Genly insists, which fosters their intimacy. An interestingly dichotomous view of sexuality seems once again to be implicit here. There is the suggestion—as in Drabble's and Laurence's fictions—that an element of sexual attraction is prerequisite to cross-gender bonding. There is an equally clear understanding, however, that this mode of relation must be handled carefully, like a delicate and dangerous explosive, lest it become destructive to the bond being established. Sexual interaction is represented as threatening to the male/female double bond since it raises the possibility of gender roles becoming once again divisive. Genly Ai and Estraven recognize clearly that to interact sexually would mean to meet once more as "aliens."

Genly and Estraven's bond is significantly enhanced by Genly's capacity for "paraverbal speech." Genly teaches Estraven this mind-speech, he says, because limitations on their ability to understand one another seem "intolerable" once his breakthrough into acceptance had occurred (249). The way in which this mental communication intensifies their bond recalls the "womb sibling" imagery referred to earlier. When Genly succeeds at last in "bespeaking" his friend, it is not Genly's voice Estraven hears but that of his dead brother Arek. Although Le Guin leaves the particulars of Estraven's relationship with his brother a mystery, the few references to Arek we are given connect him with the concept of "marriage," of yin/yang balance, which is the novel's central theme. An example is Estraven's reciting of "Tormer's Lay," the Gethenian ritual poem, to Genly and explaining that his brother quoted these lines in his last letter: "Light is the left hand of darkness/and darkness the right hand of light." In this way, the sibling bond with Arek is related to the marriage bond, the union of apparent opposites, "the end and the way," of which Estraven and Genly's relationship is also an expression (223).

The sibling bond between Estraven and Arek was also very clearly a lover's bond. Gethenian mores, we are told, allow for sibling incest, but not for vows of kemmering (i.e. monogamous marriage) between siblings. Thus, though Estraven and Arek are able to interact sexually, even to father/mother a child together, they are not permitted to "marry." This sibling bond in Estraven's past suggests again, I think (like the bonds between Morag and Jules, and Rose and Simon), that a delicate sexual balance must be sustained for transcendent bonding to be possible. Of his bond with Arek, Estraven tells Ashe that the "only true vow of faithfulness" he ever made "was not spoken . . . and the promise [was] broken, long ago" (75).

Yet the promised bond, the marriage of siblings, is achieved through Estraven's bond with Genly Ai. The exile of each is eased by the connection: Genly's exile from full selfhood and from full relationship with others because of his limiting gender constructs; Estraven's by virtue of his separation from his lost lover/brother Arek. Through mind-speech, the three are brought together. Genly is heard as Arek, Arek as Genly, linked in and with the mind of Estraven.

It is no surprise, then, when Estraven is shot by border guards and cries out "Arek!" in mindspeech, that Genly perceives this cry as meant for himself as well. In this way "he answered my love for him," Genly says (234). Genly/Arek has become, in relation to Estraven, the lost brother, the other self so close as to share the same thoughts, the other become the self.

Like Le Guin's *The Left Hand of Darkness*, Dorothy Bryant's *The Kin of Ata Are Waiting for You* (1971) seems to seek out and explore a space in which the cultural constructs which divide one individual from another may be healed. As in most of the fictions I've examined, these divisions involve more than gender. In Bryant's fiction, a broad range of divisions are challenged: the distinction between dream and reality, divisions based upon class, race, age, language, even time. Yet here, too, the central division of gender is the focus, or rather the medium, for this wider-ranging project.

Kin of Ata's narrator is its male protagonist whose role is to grapple with and learn from the alien culture in which he finds himself. Here, too (as in Le Guin's novel), it is the male character's transformation as a result of this exposure which defines the novel's central development. And it is again a double bond with another, across the boundary of gender, which makes possible this transformation.

The male protagonist is described variously as "that rare man . . . who had gotten everything he wanted" (24), as "what all men wanted to be—God help them" (26), and as "a thoroughly lost, dislocated man" (55). His characterization is, in many ways, intensely stereotypical, representing the worst in sexist, racist, and materialist ways of perceiving and relating to others. These apparently contradictory descriptions—the suggestions of "ideal manhood," the blatant sexism and inhumanity, the "everyman" aspect of the characterization suggested by the man's namelessness—implies that the ideals of masculinity are at odds with the ideals of communal cooperation, peace, and spiritual development which the utopian culture of Ata represents. That the male character is completely transformed by his experience in Ata, growing from a confused and often rebellious student to teacher, suggests a profound authorial optimism about the individual's capacity for transcending divisions, given sufficient opportunity.

The central female character, Augustine, functions as model and mentor for the male character, challenging and helping to alter all the stereotypical assumptions he brings with him to Ata from his destructive "real-world" life as a successful writer of "pulp" novels. The religious connotations of Augustine's name, of course, significantly reflect her primary role as spiritual guide for the male character, as well as for the rest of Ata. *Kin of Ata*'s central theme is, in fact, profoundly spiritual: the Atans literally "live for the dream," organizing their lives around what is "nagdeo," or conducive of enlightening dreams, and believing that listening to and following dreams is the way to spiritual enlightenment. The entire function of Ata, we are told, is to keep the world from teetering over the brink of destruction by means of their dream-oriented life and by the occasional self-selection of one of their members to return to the world as temporary guide (and often martyr).

Since dreams are central to the Atan way of life (and thus to the central spiritual theme of the novel), the double bond between Augustine and the male character is enacted most significantly in this way. From the beginning of the narrative, Augustine and the male character make contact via shared dreams; it is a connection which becomes more frequent and intense as their bond deepens, and as the man himself learns to "live for the dream." Augustine has a dream, for instance, foretelling the man's arrival in Ata—of a "howl from a creature not human . . . " which she rescues from the ocean and which then falls upon her on the sand and turns into a man. This parallels the man's "death" experience (preceding his movement into Ata), when in the "sure horror of knowing" that death was imminent, certain that it would be "a permanent plunge into the nightmare," he lets out "a great howl" (5).

This initial dream prophesies the man's transformation from one who lives separate from, and hostile to, others into one who is a spiritual guide himself by means of his writing about Ata: "The man turned his head to look at us, and turned the bright light upon us, lighting up the people of Ata so that they could be seen by the many people who stood behind" (71–72).

It is important to note how incapable of genuine connection with another human being, especially a female, the man is at the outset. His first interaction with Augustine is, in fact, an attempted rape, during which he utters such stereotypically sexist remarks as "let's not play coy" and "you're not exactly a virgin" (53–54). He describes the Atans as a race of "primitive, mental retardants"; their simple language as one of "poverty"; the peaceful quiet of their lives as "excruciating boredom" (47); and their lack of sexual roles as completely baffling. His only interest in their culture initially is to make off with the "precious gems" he sees during their ritual dances (a materialist illusion, as it turns out) and to get back to the world with the booty.

Most familiar with egotistical self-seeking and with divisions from (and among) others, he attempts to disrupt the peaceful unity of Ata by praising the limitless materialist pleasures of the "civilized" world to the Atan young people, in hopes of enlisting their aid in getting back to it. This is the arrogant and solipsistic position from which the male character begins his transformative growth. And it is from this vantage point that we perceive the uniqueness of Atan culture. As in Le Guin's novel, the male character's gradual overcoming of gender-constrained perception frees him to experience a fuller humanness and more fully to share in the unity of Atan life.

The tenor of the dreams he and Augustine share marks the progressive stages in his transformation. As the male character begins to live more in accord with what is nagdeo, his dreams reflect his growth. At first, the purpose of his dreams seems to be a playing out, and finally an overcoming, of gender division and its attendant sexual/political strife. His interaction with Augustine on the "real" plane and his dreamlife explorations of that interaction punctuate one another in cataloguing the process of his unfolding consciousness. An example is the dream he has reflecting his daily struggle to overcome a confusion of love with ownership.

A central problem in his developing relationship with Augustine is his inability to perceive of love in other than sexual/political terms. He misinterprets her words of bonding with him, that she "would be woman to you" as meaning "you are my woman," to which she responds, "I am not your woman. No one belongs to anyone" (109). The sexual script with which he is familiar is no longer functional, and he feels himself "in danger of losing some kind of struggle, losing because there was no struggle" (110). Never feeling that he "possessed her completely" (119), he accuses her frequently of not loving him, an accusation to which, once he explains what he means by love, Augustine can offer no reassuring response. When this sexual/political conflict reaches the crisis point, the man has a dream of being in the world again with an "anonymous" blonde young woman. They are arguing, and the woman is gesticulating and crying "you don't love me" over and over again, in a mewling parody of his own frustrations. As the woman prances back and forth, as if on a burlesque runway, she appears to shrink and grow younger "until she was a whining infant." After this dream, when he began to complain to Augustine, he saw the whining lover of his dream and found his own words "too funny to continue" (119). Relinquishing the destructive pattern of power-defined sexual relationship is necessary for the male character to be prepared for the gender-transcendent bond with Augustine—very like the psychic preparation both Jane and Rochester had to accomplish before their "perfect accord" could be established.

Gender constraints go deeper, however, than the sexual/political warfare expressed on the level of daily interaction, as Charlotte Brontë made clear a century before. They extend deep into the self, and the next significant dream, a climactic one in the male character's quest toward self-understanding, recounts its enactment at a deeper psychic level.

During a winter dream, the man dances the "dance of the numbers," an Atan ritual dance which describes the mystical significance of numbers, and their essential unity, as a group of twelve dancers gradually evolves and unifies into one dancer. In his dream, the man plays every dancer's part himself, all the twelve dancers representing aspects of his fragmented identity, shadows from the recurrent nightmare which brought him seeking to Ata. "They were all me, in one rotten form after another," the man says, every one fighting not to be thrown into the fire at the center and screaming in the pain of consumption by it. After what seems an eternity, only two selves are left, one male, one female, engaged in a dance of which every movement was "a threat, an aggression demanding simultaneous reaction and defense." He thinks, "I had to destroy her," but his every move is countered in a continual back and forth, attack-and-defend pattern. Finally he stops doing anything but defensive, complementary moves, "[letting] her dictate the dance." The dream woman's movements become less threatening, more neutral, as he continues to follow her until they become "great sweeps of grace, of joy, that [he] followed in perfect simultaneity as she turned darker, darker, black," until she becomes recognizable as Augustine (129–30). Together, clasped in each other's arms, they fall into the fire, merging into one.

In the dream-reality terms of Ata, appearance in a dream is actual experience; thus, Augustine suggests the next morning that he rest from work, since "it is not every winter that a man dances the numbers dance to its finish and comes out of the pit as one." To his questioning look, she responds, "Was I not there with you? Did I not jump into the fire with you when you called? I will always, always be with you when you call" (130–31).

The male character thus overcomes the internalized gender constraints which have fragmented his sense of identity, dividing him from a unified sense of self. Through his interaction with Augustine, his effort to move in complementarity with her and to see through her eyes, he becomes able both to perceive himself in greater wholeness and to connect more fully with another.

After this breakthrough dream, the male character and Augustine more often inhabit dream space together, sharing an even deeper psychic bond. Their bond becomes less physically defined, more spiritually and subconsciously sustained. For seven years after Augustine is "chosen" to return to the world, the man maintains a dream connection with her, following her movements as she goes from country to country scrubbing floors for the wealthy, singing in storefront churches, and aiding the oppressed. As he learns to become a "strong dreamer," necessary to maintain the dream-connection with Augustine, he too becomes one who "lives for the dream" and develops a compassion for humanity he had never before felt. Watching those who surround Augustine in the world, he comes to understand that "everything they did, however perverted, was truly, if they only knew it, a misdirected attempt to regain Ata. . . . I could feel nothing but pity for them . . . and even love" (196).

Of these seven years of shared dream experience, sometimes in Ata, more often in the world, the man says "we learned to be together in almost every instant, and we rose to love which shares pain" (198). He is present at her death, when she is shot during a street riot, and even after her death, he feels her "essence . . . in the air, in the people, the animals, something that was and was not Augustine, but was becoming something greater than Augustine, something purer, now that she was released" (203).

When he is also chosen to return to the world, to fulfill Augustine's dream-prophecy of "shining a light" on Ata through the book he writes about his experience there (to be followed very shortly by his death), he still feels her presence and guidance as "a small black moth" (moths and butterflies being always associated with Augustine) flutters down to light upon his shoulder. He experiences an overwhelming sense of unity as he attests to Ata's existence and refuses to deny past actions: "Light was everywhere. . . . I was full and whole. I was part of the light and of all the other things that shone in and with the light. All were one. And whole" (218).

By the end of the narrative, the male protagonist shares the Atan perception, reflected in the purity of their language, of now being the only time, there being no past or future; of all human beings as, not he or she, but simply "kin," sex, race, age, and class both various and irrelevant; of dream and reality as only different dimensions of the same truth of being; and of death as only a going "Home" which imposes no barrier to connection. The only division which remains is that between those pursuing the Atan way of spiritual development and those unaware of their desire for it. Even this barrier, however, is described as essentially superficial, it being only a matter of time (though perhaps a very long time) before everyone comes back to Ata. Clearly, the male/female double of Bryant's *The Kin of Ata Are Waiting for You* is an image of transcendence, not only of gender division, but also of numerous other divisive constructs in human perception.

The same can be said of the double in James Tiptree Jr.'s fiction. The story of Alice Sheldon's long and successful literary disguise as James Tiptree Jr., and the shock of revelation which attended its conclusion, served as a useful reminder (to those of us who needed reminding) that gender is still, for many readers, a prime consideration in the assessment of writing. Ursula LeGuin, in her introduction to Tiptree's *Star Songs of an Old Primate*, almost chortles over the "beautiful Jill-in-the-box" way Tiptree "fooled us good and proper," and muses on the kind of "psychic bias" that led one noted science fiction writer (Robert Silverberg) to assert: "It has been suggested that Tiptree is a female, a theory that I find absurd, for there is to me something ineluctably masculine about Tiptree's writing" (xii). It is an age-old bias, of course, one with which Charlotte and Emily Brontë were on equally familiar terms. And in both cases—though separated by over a hundred years—the pseudonymous impulse expresses the same resistance to gender-based pigeonholing, the same desire for self-expression regardless of gender.

As with other female fantasy/science fiction writers, Tiptree's fiction is significantly concerned with the divisions of gender and the "psychic bias" which such division fosters. Tiptree's fictional perspective on sexual difference and sexually prescribed ways of perceiving and ordering existence, is for the most part extremely grim, however. Indeed, hostility between the sexes, and the link between aggression and eroticism, are represented in much of Tiptree's fiction as virtual biological imperatives. As Lillian Heldreth sums it up, "Tiptree seems to see no hope for feminist equality, no release from the bondage of violent sex, and no hope for the human race" (28).

This was the case, at least, until publication of her first novel (after ten years of writing shorter fictions), *Up the Walls of the World* (1978). This panoramic "space opera" is both her most ambitious fiction and her most optimistic one. Tiptree created in this novel not just an alternative world or a utopian society, but an entirely new galaxy, even galaxies, in incipient form. Thus, as in the other fictions I have examined, her effort to transcend cultural divisions, though using gender as a focus, also goes far beyond gender.

The narrative is enacted on three levels: the "Destroyer," a vast interstellar computer being gone awry, destroying all suns in its path; the planet Tyree, which is inhabited by a race of telepathic, flying beings (and which is in the path of the Destroyer); and contemporary Earth, with a government-funded group of ESP researchers. The interconnection of life forms, or of energic forms (physicality itself being cast off in this fictional space) on all three levels is the focus of the narrative, and the means by which a variety of divisions are overcome.

In a sense, Tiptree's novel does not contradict the perspective of her earlier fictions that feminist equality is impossible. Earth and Tyree are, after all, alternative versions of a similar patriarchal reality. Though among Tyrennians men bear and nurture the young, and women lead lives of work, travel, and adventure, here too, whatever is masculine carries higher status. Fathering is regarded as almost a sacred task (the word "Father" is always capitalized), and, except for a few "radical feminists" like Avanil, women are accustomed to being excluded from this more important dimension of life. Instead, Tiptree's novel simply renders the issue of female-male equality a moot point, taking us into a space where gender, and physicality itself, become irrelevant.

It is from the perspective of Dr. Daniel Dann, medical assistant to the Earth ESP research group, that much of the narrative is told. Keenly sensitive to the pain of others, because of his own painful past (which he stays drugged to keep from remembering), he is the receiver of the Tyrennian Giadoc's far-reaching consciousness, who is, by the order of a group of Fathers, sent to discover if inhabiting alien life forms would be an escape from their doom. Dann's unique receptivity to the consciousness of others, and thus his suitability as Giadoc's contact, is strikingly represented in his interaction with the group's computer specialist, Margaret Omali. Dann and Omali's highly interactive mental bond is another example of the male/female double.

A significant part of this interaction is a sharing of memories. In the charged atmosphere created by the alien contact of extending Tyree consciousness and the ESP subjects' unique sensitivities, Dann and Omali experience a spontaneous exchange of their most painful memories. Dann suddenly feels himself "swamped by dreadfulness," and mentally experiences the sexual mutilation at the hands of her father which Margaret had experienced as a girl. "A knife shines above him. Mother! Mother! Help me! But there is no help, the unspeakable blade is forced between his young legs. . . . But as he clasps his gushing crotch he feels alien structure, understands that he is female. His childish body has breasts, his knees are dark-skinned." Margaret, at the same time, experiences the "unceasing nightmare" of Dann's life, the fire in which his wife and baby died: "'The fire,' she whispers intensely. . . . 'The fire,' 'Burning—the baby—Mary. Mary! Oh-h-h-'. . . . I should have gone back . . . I should" (100). Like the shared dreams of Bryant's characters, the male/female pair here express their bond via shared consciousness, shared memory. Its effect is a partial merging of identity which culminates in their final merging (along with other humans and Tyrennians) in the "body" of the Destroyer.

This merging of identity across the boundary of gender occurs between other pairs of characters as well, as when Tivonel merges with Giadoc (the Tyrennian version of Dann and Omali) in order to save his life. "Opening her life-energy to his," she gives him "the ultimate Tyrenni gift. . . . Their fields merge and the life-current flows" (251). Elsewhere, Dann merges with the ESP subject Val in an attempt to reassure her after the consciousness transfer to Tyree. Not having yet adequate control of his telepathic "field " he "literally falls through her mind" and finds himself experiencing another individual's reality as his own: "A world named Val, a strange vivid landscape in space and time, composed of a myriad familiar scenes, faces, voices, objects, musics, body sensations, memories, experiences—all centered round his Val-self." Since central to Val's self is her lesbianism, Dann experiences this reality as well, recalling a scene in which "on his/her/my naked stomach is resting an intimately known head of brown hair. A head which is We Love—is a complex of tenderness, ambiguous resentments, sweet sharing, doubts, worry" . . . within "a frail enchanted space outside which looms the injustice called daily life" (216). Coming back to himself, Dann feels transformed: "He is not himself; not as he was nor ever will be again. For the first time he has really grasped life's most eerie lesson: The Other Exists" (217). Having experienced, as his own, another human reality, the boundary between self and other has become blurred and can never again be perceived as absolute, impermeable. The other exists and has a reality as true and complete as one's own. A purer example of collapsed gender barriers can hardly be imagined.

Clearly more than one "double" is represented in Tiptree's novel, and more than one type of division transcended. Consciousness in general is shown to be remarkably permeable, and highly interactive. Divisions between different species are traversable, as Tyrenni and Terrestrial beings alternate forms, communicate telepathically, and exchange memories. Vast distances in space and time are crossed by the seeking consciousnesses of individuals from both Earth and Tyree. The barrier of physicality itself is overcome. "The mind is all, it really is" (217), Dr. Dann says after his experience with Val, and this seems to be borne out by the image with which the novel concludes, of an interactive multiplicity of disembodied consciousnesses. Transported by Giadoc off the burning planet of Tyree and into the massive space being, The Destroyer, all that is left of the group of Tyrenni and human beings are the colorful, fluctuating "energy fields" of their consciousnesses. And they have all, in a sense, merged with (or inside) the Destroyer via the "computer consciousness" of Margaret Omali which has become somehow contained within its nucleus.

The psychic connection between Dann and Omali is instrumental in effecting this harmonious union. Dann lends his psychic energy in her effort to negate the destructive program of the Destroyer, his being the only consciousness she will allow to make contact. She, in fact, requires his assistance as "gatekeeper," as intermediary between life forms and computer essence, in order to alter the Destroyer's path.

The imagery of the scene is of hands extending toward a "giant busbar" on a computer console (though, in their disembodied state, they are only "psychic hands" reaching) and of Dann merging his energy with Omali's: "It is dizzying, transcendent, transsexual—he hugs, tugs recklessly, opening his very life to her need, pressing himself into her, giving himself to convert to the power of her grip." Their blended energies, though the crucial connection, are not enough, however. Dann calls for help from those waiting behind, and "help comes; surging up through him like a violent sharp wave washing through to the nexus where he holds her, to the crucial point where she holds the unknowable. It's intoxicating, a renewal of life mingled of human and Tyrenni essence intertwined" (272). All sense of individual consciousness is lost.

This multiplicity of space-borne consciousnesses—human, Tyrenni, and undefined space being linked with Omali—converts the "Destroyer" into the "Saver." The individual beings contained within the

Saver's great mass, Tivonel says, are likely to get "more like each other with all this mind-touching" (306); thus individual consciousness is likely to become more and more diffuse. At the novel's end, this immense consciousness is in the process of devising a new "task" for the Saver, which may include rescuing more "aliens" from extinction on dying planets or founding new worlds. Thus it ends with a new beginning, for a new race, on an eternal journey through space. The extensive blending of consciousness involved in the novel's closing scenes makes clear the extent to which divisions of all kinds are transcended in Tiptree's novel. The brief, closing "Destroyer" chapter sums up neatly this image of multiplicity in oneness, transcending all divisions between one being and another: "It is a proto-pronoun, an it becoming she becoming they, a we becoming I which is becoming mystery" (310).

In the end, Tiptree's novel suggests that the division of gender is itself a nexus, a crucial boundary to cross before other kinds of transcendence become possible. It suggests as well—like the fictions of Bryant, Le Guin, Laurence, even Woolf—that crossing this boundary is a matter of survival. In order to alter the destructive path of the huge Destroyer we have created (with its hints of NASA origins, "ghost programs," and so on), we must learn to transcend not only the constraints of gender, but of individual consciousness itself.

Tiptree's fiction presents an optimistic view of the possibilities for human renewal—and an equally optimistic view of gender. Though it can divide (and all these writers are aware of its constraints), gender can also be used to advantage, they seem to suggest, in helping us to overcome the divisiveness of our own perceptions of ourselves and others. As Le Guin describes this perspective in *The Left Hand of Darkness*, gender itself can be "the bridge, the only bridge, across what divide[s] us."

Conclusion

In different contexts and according to different methods, all the fictions I have examined demonstrate what appears to me a remarkably optimistic perspective on gender. They suggest not only that men and women, given the appropriate space, can transcend the divisive boundaries of gender to interact in new and deeper ways, but also that gender difference itself can be used to constructive ends.

All the writers make clear in their fictions an awareness of the restrictiveness of gender—and a clear sense that it is, given social realities, not likely to go away. This knowledge is reflected certainly in the nature of the male/female doubles they create and the space in which they are situated. There seems, in effect, to be a general agreement that a male/female bond like that of Brontë's Catherine and Heathcliff can only exist outside social space, on the fringes of the "civilized" world, its "natural" place being somehow more mythically than socially realizable.

These writers also suggest, however, that, despite this reality, an approach to gender difference can be found which defies its constraints and expands the self. Charlotte Brontë perhaps defines this project, showing Jane Eyre and Rochester goading one another into transcending the internalized restrictions of gender, thus into fuller growth, in their effort to achieve an equal marriage. Virginia Woolf carves out "beautiful caves" behind her characters, Clarissa and Septimus, revealing how, on a deep psychic plane, they reflect one another's self, one another's reality, in a way which transcends divisions not only between male and female, but also between sanity and insanity, survival and death. Margaret Drabble describes Simon Camish's development, into something approaching "grace" through contact with the "otherness" of Rose Vassiliou, through "[wanting] what she is" and making that something part of himself. Margaret Laurence, approaching this constructive male-female interaction from the opposite side, describes how the female artist, Morag Gunn, is bolstered and enabled by interaction with the otherness of her "male muse." And the three science fiction writers I have discussed reveal how, in the wider expanses of fantasy, gender not only can be transcended to allow fuller growth for men and women, but it can be a "way in" to the confrontation of a wide array of cultural divisions, all of which, in the contexts of utopias, alien planets, and interplanetary space, can be healed.

All social evidence to the contrary, in effect, these fictions project an image of gender as remarkably malleable, and finally quite superficial. Given recent theoretical work on female writers' attitudes toward gender, this should not surprise us. As Sandra M. Gilbert explains in her article, "Costumes of the Mind," women writers have long projected a more "fluid" image of gender and its superficial "costumes" and have often attempted in their fictions to strip such costumes away "to reveal the pure, sexless (or third-sexed) being behind gender" (215). For the female writer, Gilbert asserts, "an ultimate reality exists only if one journeys beyond gender" (196). Since it is more often those who are on the short end of limiting social strictures who are most aware of their falsity, it makes sense that women writers might have a keener awareness of the essential falsehood of gender as a way of defining and expressing the self. Thus the fictions I have examined portray gender as something which can be stripped away to reveal an essential sameness or connection.

As these fiction writers strive to "journey beyond gender," they also attempt to transcend numerous other cultural divisions which separate being from being, being from nature, even being from deity. In most of the fictions, gender emerges finally as a metaphor for division, for separateness, and for polarity in human life generally. Woolf, for example, voicing her distress over "life's power to divide": though she uses (and certainly sees) gender as a focal point, a central expression of this reality, her concern with division transcends this category alone. Similarly, Drabble suggests that the division of gender is somehow akin to separation from grace; and Laurence's fiction posits that for the female artist, connection with the masculine is creative necessity.

Contemporary writers of science fiction and fantasy take this metaphor further still. Le Guin, Bryant, and Tiptree all represent gender as a significant division between human beings, but use it also as a medium through which to confront numerous other polarities, separations, schisms in human life. Le Guin's "thought-experiment," for example— a perfect example of Gilbert's assertion regarding women writers' pursuit of a "genderless" state—describes how Genly Ai's overcoming of his "gender blinders" allows for an intensely interactive connection with Estraven, and how this is (with its womb imagery) virtually a rebirth. Bryant stretches the metaphor further, suggesting, with her male/female bond, the centrality of transcending gender constraints to the development of spiritual enlightenment, and to, finally, the redemption of culture. And Tiptree's vision, at once more grim and most exuberant, suggests that getting beyond the divisions of gender is a crucial link (as in the connection between Dann and Omali at the "Destroyer" console) in arresting the destructive path of culture. It is the first important step toward the greater transcendence of individual consciousness itself which, it seems, is the only hope for humankind. The image of wholeness and unity with which Tiptree's novel concludes, the "protopronoun," makes clear the potential power of transcending gender constraints which such fiction writers perceive—and the way in which gender serves metaphorically to represent infinitely greater and deeper divisions in human life.

All the fictions I have examined, from Brontë to Tiptree, share this vision of the potential power of gender, not as restriction, but as metaphorical agent for radical social change. Though the image is most pure in those fictions situated outside conventional social space, even in the "realistic" fictions I have discussed, one can still glimpse Catherine and Heathcliff "haunting" authorial consciousness, looming up in the background to suggest what a disturbingly different world we would inhabit were the divisions of life with which we are familiar to be dispelled. The authorial attitude toward this power for change, through the breakdown of gender polarity, ranges from ambivalence (as in Emily Brontë's *Wuthering Heights*) to, in the fantasy fictions, a kind of exaltation. But all the fictions here project a vision, though faint at times, of a greater wholeness, and a greater power, which might become operative in human life when the boundary which separates male and female is challenged.

There is a gender-transcendent, or more accurately perhaps, a "genderless" reality underlying even the least "fantastic" fictions I have discussed. It seems then appropriate to reexamine the mythic terrain of the Andersen tale to see how it enhances our understanding of the male/female doubles which are central to these fictions.

The Kay/Gerda double of "The Snow Queen" illustrates a number of the characteristics· of the male/female double. The tale suggests, for instance, the importance of the male-female connection, that neither self is successful or complete when separated from the other. It reflects the idea (echoed by several of the fictions) that the feminine perspective, with its culturally developed emphasis on sustaining human relations, can be particularly advantageous in transcending divisions. And it affirms that the central point about male/female bonding is not who achieves it, or how it is achieved, but that the connection be made—and that this united force (since, after Kay and Gerda's reunion, the land "flourishes") is potentially redemptive.

The fictions I have examined here seem to suggest that gender is itself like the shattered mirror of "The Snow Queen" in that it fragments and distorts our perceptions of ourselves, of each other, and of the world around us. They suggest that if we could manage somehow—and it is likely to be, like Gerda's trek to the wild north, a long, laborious journey—to put those fragments together and to see the mirror whole, we might discover a new and better reflection of human life. We might, once we have healed its divisions, gaze into that mirror of gender to perceive that the face of the other inside it is only a reflection of our own.

Notes

Introduction

1. Charlotte Goodman, in "The Lost Brother, The Twin: Women Novelists and The Male-Female Double Bildungsroman," discusses a male/female double in fictions of development by Brontë, Eliot, Cather, Stafford, and Oates. Her assertion that such male-female relationships "suggest the possibility of androgynous wholeness, a state imaginable only in a mythic prelapsarian world of nature before a patriarchal culture gained ascendancy" (31) is concurrent with my view of the difficulties of social placement such fiction writers encounter. I question the accuracy of "androgyny" as definition of such "doubles," however, and believe they are evident in a wider range of women's fictions, the bildungsroman being among them.

2. A useful overview of the criticism on androgyny is provided by Barbara Charlesworth Gelpi, Cynthia Secor, and Daniel A. Harris.

3. Some interesting revisions of androgyny can be found in S. L. Bem, R. Hefner, M. Rebecca, Barbara Oleshansky, and Janet T. Spence.

4. On the tradition of the double, see Albert J. Guerard, C. F. Keppler, R. D. Laing, Morris Beja, Otto Rank, Robert Rogers, and Ralph Tymms.

5. In a similar vein, Judith Fetterley describes the way in which women readers, because of the masculine bias of American fiction, are compelled to identify against the negative female characters in these fictions, and thus against themselves.

6. In an investigation of heterosexual and lesbian love in women's fiction, Annis Pratt argues that in those few novels wherein Eros is not destructive for the heroes, it is situated "in a new, inevitably apatriarchal space" (74).

Chapter 1

1. On the Jane/Bertha double in *Jane Eyre,* see Gilbert and Gubar, Rigney, and Showalter.

2. Gilbert and Gubar discuss *Wuthering Heights'* apparent reversal of Miltonian myth, in which, rather than a fall into hell, "a fall from 'hell' into 'heaven'" (255) is represented.

3. Gilbert and Gubar note the anorexic parallels between Catherine's and Heathcliff's near death experiences, using these as partial evidence for their interesting (if somewhat problematic) argument for Heathcliff's essential "femaleness."

4. Contemporary reviews of *Wuthering Heights* communicated a sense of moral outrage. The *Spectator* found Emily Brontë's "incidents and persons . . . too coarse and disagreeable to be attractive," though conceded "the execution, however, is good" (December 18, 1847). The *Quarterly Review*, which did not acknowledge the novel until a year after its publication, said that "with all the unscrupulousness of the French school of novels it combines that repulsive vulgarity in the choice of its vice which supplies its own antidote," and that it could not have been written by a woman—except perhaps by one who had "long forfeited the society of her own sex" (December, 1848). The *North American Review* (October 1848), commenting on the work of the Brontës in general, called it an "attempt to corrupt the virtue of the sturdy descendants of the Puritans."

5. See Elizabeth Cleghorn Gaskell, Clement K. Shorter, and Norma Crandall (the latter critic's contention that Emily Brontë's relationship with brother Branwell provided the emotional locus for *Wuthering Heights* renders her text too idiosyncratic to be reliable—a problem with much of the biographical material available on Brontë—but the information it provides on Brontë's habitually reclusive and independent lifestyle is useful).

6. Q. D. Leavis, introduction to *Jane Eyre* (New York: Penguin, 1966), 13.

7. See Showalter, Rigney, and Rich.

8. Gail B. Griffin argues that the gypsy scene is significant for its representation of Rochester as transcending his own gender and "submerging himself in his female identity." Because of this submersion, Griffin claims, "he can know her not as Other but with the knowledge that comes of identification, of projection of the self into another—a knowledge particularly feminine and unlike his customary arrogant assertions of mental mastery" (121).

9. In her discussion of the psychosexual dynamics at work in the Jane-Rochester relationship, Helene Moglen emphasizes Rochester's fear of the female, both within and without, which is imposed first on Bertha, and then on Jane. Moglen argues that Bertha Mason symbolizes both Jane's and Rochester's ambivalence toward romantic bonding.

10. Nancy Pell uses this quote as her rubric for an analysis of the extent to which *Jane Eyre* is structured by "an underlying social and economic critique of bourgeois patriarchal authority" (399).

Chapter 2

1. Some recent feminist literary criticism focusing on androgyny, such as by Carolyn Heilbrun and Nancy Topping Bazin, has contributed to this misunderstanding by extending Woolf's aesthetic model into a social context, an extension which, given Woolf's explicitly aesthetic context, is problematic.

2. Elizabeth Abel, M. Hirsch, and E. Langland, in *The Voyage In: Fictions of Female Development*, use Woolf's *The Voyage Out* as a focal point for their discussion of the

female developmental story and describe this inward movement as one of its central characteristics.

3. Abel, in "Narrative Structure(s) and Female Development: The Case of *Mrs. Dalloway*," elucidates that problematic schism between past and present in the developmental story of Clarissa Dalloway. Septimus Warren Smith, because of his wartime experience, reflects a similar gap in personal history.

4. Also in "Narrative Structure(s) and Female Development," Abel clarifies the important connection between Woolf's developmental story in *Mrs. Dalloway* and the feminine developmental theories of Freud, which were developed concurrently.

5. *Jacob's Room* holograph notebook, Berg Collection; as quoted in Phyllis Rose, *Woman of Letters: A Life of Virginia Woolf*.

6. See Abel ("Narrative Structure(s) and Female Development") and Rose on the recurrent images of "threads and webs" which in *Mrs. Dalloway* symbolize "the creativity of everyday feminine life" of which "the goal is connection" (Rose, 130). The association with Gilligan's suggestion about women's "network of connections" is also apparent.

Works Cited

Primary Sources

Andersen, Hans Christian. "The Snow Queen." *Andersen's Fairy Tales*. New York: Grosset & Dunlap, 1945.

Brontë, Charlotte. *Jane Eyre*. New York: Penguin, 1966.

Brontë, Emily. *Wuthering Heights*. New York: Collier, 1962.

Bryant, Dorothy. *The Kin of Ata Are Waiting for You*. New York: Moon Books/Random House, 1971.

Drabble, Margaret. *The Needle's Eye*. New York: Popular Library, 1972.

Laurence, Margaret. *Heart of a Stranger*. Toronto: McClelland & Stewart, 1976.

——— . *The Diviners*. Toronto: McClelland & Stewart, 1974.

——— . *The Fire Dwellers*. New York: Popular Library, 1969.

——— . *The Stone Angel*. Toronto: McClelland & Stewart, 1964.

Le Guin, Ursula K. *The Language of the Night: Essays on Fantasy and Science Fiction*. Ed. Susan Wood. New York: Berkley, 1979.

——— . *The Left Hand of Darkness*. New York: Ace, 1969.

Tiptree, James Jr. *Up the Walls of the World*. New York: Berkley, 1978.

Woolf, Virginia. *A Writer's Diary*. Ed. Leonard Woolf. New York: Harcourt Brace Jovanovich, 1953.

——— . *A Room of One's Own*. New York: Harcourt Brace Jovanovich, 1929.

——— . "Jane Eyre and Wuthering Heights." In *The Common Reader*, 161–63. New York: Harcourt Brace and World, 1925.

——— . *Mrs. Dalloway*. New York: Penguin, 1925.

——— . *Night and Day*. New York: Harcourt Brace Jovanovich, 1919.

——— . *The Voyage Out*. New York: Harcourt Brace Jovanovich, 1915.

Secondary Sources

Abel, Elizabeth. "Narrative Structure(s) and Female Development: The Case of Mrs. Dalloway." *The Voyage In: Fictions of Female Development*, 161–85. Eds. Elizabeth Abel, M. Hirsch, and E. Langland. Hanover: University Press of New England, 1983.

Bazin, Nancy Topping. *Virginia Woolf and the Androgynous Vision*. New Brunswick: Rutgers University Press, 1973.

Beja, Morris. Ed. *Psychological Fiction*. Glenview, Ill.: Scott Foresman, 1971.

Bem, S. L. "Beyond Androgyny." *The Psychology of Women: Future Directions of Research*. Eds. J. A. Sherman and F. L. Denmark. New York: Psychological Dimensions, Inc., 1978.

Bloom, Harold. *Anxiety of Influence*. New York: Oxford University Press, 1973.

Chodorow, Nancy. *The Reproduction of Mothering: Psychoanalysis and the Sociology of Gender*. Berkeley: University of California Press, 1978.

Crandall, Norma. *Emily Brontë: A Psychological Portrait*. Topside, N. H.: Smith, 1957.

Fetterley, Judith. *The Resisting Reader: A Feminist Approach to American Fiction*. Bloomington: Indiana University Press, 1977.

Gaskell, Elizabeth Cleghorn. *The Life of Charlotte Brontë*. London: J. M. Dent, 1908.

Gelpi, Barbara Charlesworth. "The Politics of Androgyny." *Women's Studies* 2 (1974): 151–60.

Gilbert, Sandra M. "Costumes of the Mind." In *Writing and Sexual Difference*, 193–220. Chicago: University of Chicago Press, 1980.

Gilbert, Sandra M. and Susan Gubar. *The Madwoman in the Attic*. New Haven: Yale University Press, 1979.

Gilligan, Carol. *In a Different Voice: Psychological Theory and Women's Development*. Cambridge: Harvard University Press, 1982.

Goodman, Charlotte. "The Lost Brother, The Twin: Women Novelists and the Male-Female Double Bildungsroman." *Novel: A Forum on Fiction* 17, no. 1 (Fall 1983): 28–43.

Griffin, Gail B. "The Humanization of Edward Rochester." *Women and Literature*. Vol. 2 n.s.: *Men by Women*, 118–29. Ed. Janet Todd. New York: Holmes and Meier, 1982.

Guerard, Albert J. "Concepts of the Double." In *Stories of the Double*. Ed. Albert J. Guerard. New York: J. B. Lippincott, 1967.

Hacker, Helen. "Women as a Minority Group." *Social Forces* 30 (October 1951): 60–69.

Hardin, Nancy S. "An Interview With Margaret Drabble." *The Southern Review*. 14, no. 3 (July 1973).

Harris, Daniel A. "Androgyny: The Sexist Myth in Disguise." *Women's Studies* 2 (1974): 171–84.

Hefner, R., M. Rebecca, and Barbara Oleshansky. "Development of Sex-Role Transcendence." *Human Development* 18 (1975): 143–58.

Heilbrun, Carolyn. *Toward a Recognition of Androgyny*. New York: Knopf, 1973.

Heldreth, Lillian M. "'Love Is the Plan, the Plan Is Death': The Feminism and Fatalism of James Tiptree Jr." *Extrapolation* 23, no. 1 (Spring 1982).

Keppler, C. F. *The Literature of the Second Self*. Tucson: University of Arizona Press, 1972.

Laing, R. D. *The Divided Self*. London: Tavistock, 1960.

Memmi, Albert. *Dominated Man: Notes toward a Portrait*. New York: Orion Press, 1968.

Miller, Jean Baker. *Toward a New Psychology of Women*. Boston: Beacon Press, 1976.

Moglen, Helene. *Charlotte Brontë: The Self Conceived*. New York: Norton, 1976.

Pell, Nancy. "Resistance, Rebellion, and Marriage: The Economics of Jane Eyre." *Nineteenth-Century Fiction* 31 (1977).

Pratt, Annis. *Archetypal Patterns in Women's Fiction*. Bloomington: Indiana University Press, 1981.

Rank, Otto. *The Double: A Psychoanalytic Study*. Chapel Hill: University of North Carolina Press, 1971.

Rich, Adrienne. "Jane Eyre: The Temptations of a Motherless Woman." In *On Lies, Secrets and Silence*. New York: Norton, 1979.

Rigney, Barbara. *Madness and Sexual Politics in the Feminist Novel*. Madison: University of Wisconsin Press, 1978.

Rogers, Robert. *A Psychoanalytic Study of the Double in Literature*. Detroit: Wayne State University Press, 1970.

Rose, Phyllis. *Woman of Letters: A Life of Virginia Woolf*. New York: Oxford University Press, 1978.

Secor, Cynthia. "Androgyny: An Early Reappraisal." *Women's Studies* 2 (1974): 161–69.

Shorter, Clement K. *Charlotte Brontë and Her Sisters.* New York: Scribner's, 1905.

Showalter, Elaine. *A Literature of Their Own.* Princeton: Princeton University Press, 1977.

Silverberg, Robert. "Who Is Tiptree, What Is He?" In *Warm Worlds and Otherwise,* ix–xviii. New York: Ballantine, 1975.

Spence, Janet T. "Changing Conceptions of Men and Women." *A Feminist Perspective in the Academy.* Eds. Elizabeth Langland and Walter Gove. Chicago: University of Chicago Press, 1981.

Tymms, Ralph. *Doubles in Literary Psychology.* Cambridge: Bowes and Bowes, 1949.

Index